Journey to Love

A Memoir

Dolores Eckles

Lynette,

Be Love ♡

Dolores A. Eckles

Produced by:

FriesenPress

Suite 300 – 852 Fort Street

Victoria, BC, Canada V8W 1H8

www.friesenpress.com

Distributed to the trade by The Ingram Book Company

Table of Contents

Preface

*C*uriosity poses questions. What is love? Have you ever been in love? Were you one of the lucky ones born into a loving environment? Or are you one of the majority of us who had to learn love on your life's journey? Or is love elusive for you? Once love is learned, will it grow?

Love is connection, even with strangers. Yesterday, I had the opportunity to experience that connection three times. I had deep conversations with two persons, once strangers, during a luncheon after hearing a speaker. The second time, as I was in the parking lot of K-Mart, I noticed a young girl of about eight wearing a stylish red coat while holding her mother's hand. She turned to look at me three times. I told her she was a pretty girl in a pretty red coat. Her mother said to her that I was wearing one, too. After making a purchase inside, a lady remarked to me that she had noticed how elegant I looked in that red cape. We exchanged a few pleasantries and parted with a hug.

Love is for giving and receiving. When we live in a perpetual, heart-centered *Now*, love miracles happen frequently, for we are each Love incarnate.

An irreverent Archangel Michael, portrayed in the movie by John Travolta, belted the message in the Beatles' song "All You Need Is Love." Amen.

Dedication

TO: My Spiritual Family, You know who you are;

and

TO: My treasured daughters, Donna and Rhonda

Introduction

*W*hat is love? Have you been in love? There are as many definitions of love as those who define it. In a simple sense, love is respect and an attraction, with attendant emotions, to another being.

I am motivated to write this book by taking a session of an autobiography writing class offered at my church by a former creative writing teacher. I decided that the genre "memoir", a subset of autobiography, would be a more accurate genre for the story I wish to tell. I began research on writing this form. I consulted William Zinsser's *On Writing Well* Seventh Edition (HarperCollins: 2006), which I found on the "required reading" table at Barnes and Noble; Strunk and White's *Elements of Style* Fourth Edition (Longman: 2000); R. Brooks and B. Richardson's *You Really Should Write a Book: How to Write, Sell and Market Your Memoir* (St. Martin's Press: 2012); and Zinsser's *Writing about Your Life* (Marlowe & Company: 2004) which is an enthralling, delightful read that says, in the final five words of Chapter 10 How to Write a Memoir, "...tell your story with integrity." I raised my fisted right arm and shot it down with a resounding "Yes!"

I spent a week choosing the subject of the book; a title; a focus; chapter divisions; and the experiences I wanted to share. I downloaded an on-line author's guide provided by an assisted self-publishing source; I was telephoned by a publishing consultant from the company the next day. We chatted, and I plan the manuscript to be completed in 4-5 months.

In this memoir, reference is made to the three types of love defined by the ancient Greeks: Eros (romantic, erotic); Philos (brotherly or friendship); and Agape (unconditional or God Love) and relate my spiritual journey in learning and growing Love. About a month after I began writing, I realized a third component to learning and growing Love.

There are also other types of love, chief among them Self-Love. Writing about my memories will serve three purposes: healing my psyche; acting as a legacy for what remains of my core family; and serving as an example to others on a similar journey facing challenges that have no immediate, indefinable purpose. I seek to encourage and inspire others with my experiences and their outcomes that have made me the person I am today. I have lived seventy years and have stories to tell. If I can survive and thrive, so can you. The flow of experiences is roughly a chronological journey indicated by chapters.

I am an organized person, and I have tried to be fair and accurate in what I have written. Some situations do not warrant white-washing. Some scenarios are from memory, others are bolstered by albums of print photos (before the digital age) with index cards inserted with dates and description; an abridged resume of employment with places and dates; Internet searches; and med procedures document listings from 2007 to the present.

Writers are readers. I will be mentioning by author and title some of the dozens of books I have read on the topic of the meaning of life and meeting its challenges with strength, determination and courage. As Eleanor Roosevelt is quoted, "Courage is fear who has said her prayers." I can attest to all three ideas: courage, fear, prayers. My spirit is one of adventure.

Some ideas in this book are revolutionary, and you may not agree with them; however, I hope you find value in having read these pages. Love to each of you.

Dolores Eckles
November, 2013

1.
Childhood

"Just like a little doll; she's so cute," my mother wrote in my baby book along with weight, length, first tooth, first steps, etc.-- sweet, kind, well-liked, practical, community-service oriented, frugal mother. (Thank you, Mother, for the inheritance) Later, she saved my report cards in elementary, high school and college, along with a pair of baby shoes, news clippings, and a napkin from my senior prom. She even saved the fourth grade report card where I received a "C" in deportment (behavior). I got a "B" as the year-end grade. I was full of spunk at an early age. Most years, that category was an "A".

I was an excellent student in school. The reason may be that I was the oldest child in birth order. Dr. Kevin Leman's *The Birth Order Book: Why You Are the Way You Are* (Fleming H. Revell Company: 1985) "...shows how your position in the family shapes your personality and determines your interests and career choices." Sources detail the first born as being a leader; independent; over-achiever; has a close group of friends; perfectionist; and wants to make people happy. It is an accurate description of *moi*.

My mother loved me; I just did not know it early in life. The word "love" was never mentioned until, in my 40's and with maturity, I said, "I love you" for the first time to her over the telephone. She then began saying it to me during our conversations. Hers was a love a mother has for her first-born child. In my college years, I learned from her friends that she was proud of me, proud of my accomplishments in being the first of the cousins to graduate from college, in marrying well, and providing her with two adorable granddaughters.

Mother was born on a farm in 1920. She was an only child who worked hard doing the necessary chores. She picked cotton in the heat and humidity of central Texas summers. I remember how I hated picking cotton on my grandfather's farm with the heat and bleeding fingers from the sharp, dried bolls that encased the cotton. I wore gloves made of cotton. Picking is different from pulling. Picked cotton (just the cotton, not the boll) brought more money at the cotton gin. Adults would drag 6 ft. sacks; I had a smaller one which I dumped at the end of a row into a large trailer pulled by a tractor in the field and by a truck to bring to the cotton gin. Now there are defoliants and stripper machines that facilitate harvesting.

There were fun times on Grandpa's nearby farm — like the time I squirted milk at my brother from the udder of the cow I was milking. Making mud pies decorated with mulberry leaves and pressed out from a round tractor part was creative, if not delicious. Making bows and arrows from chinaberry trees created imagination to play cowboys and Indians. Kind Grandpa would chide us kids for locking the chickens in their coop, but he did teach us to make whistles by splitting the reverse end of a feather (the end which had been in the chicken).

I can still smell and taste the fresh homemade bread Grandma baked for our snacks, before her stroke. Chopping off a chicken's head did not faze her. The chicken was dinner. The poor bird ran around the barnyard with his neck spurting blood. It must have been painful, but I am sure that he did not feel the boiling water being poured over his feathers for plucking. The process smelled awful.

My mother's mother died when I was fifteen. She had a stroke and needed to be bathed and cared for. I think we were both embarrassed: me because of my tender age, and her because of dependence on others. This grandmother was the wife of my cherished grandfather with whom I spent the times mentioned above.

I learned later in life that Grandma would hit Mother and call her names when she was growing up. Mother had more of the same from my father after their marriage. I don't know if my mother ever heard the word "love" in her childhood, perhaps a negligent practice that went back generations.

Mother and Daddy were married in 1940. I came three years later. My brother was two years younger, and my sister was six years younger than me. My father was not called into WWII because of a serious injury when he was younger and a wagon wheel sliced his shoulder.

As siblings, the three of us were not close. After I graduated from high school, we went our separate ways.

My sister was a widow at the age of 25 when her husband was killed in a motorcycle accident. She had two small children to raise, one almost four years old and one six months old, Terry and Joey. Terry was in an accident which left him a paraplegic for 32 of his 37 years on this earth. He died in March, 2008. Joan had earlier married a good man who helped her raise the boys.

My sister smoked (I'm allergic), and she and my second husband did not get along. We rarely saw one another when living in the same state. When Mother died in 2002 at the age of 82, Joan was the Executrix of her estate. Joan worked hard to do the work which needed to be done. It was shortly after Mother died that my elder daughter Donna suggested that Joan and I were each who we are and to accept each as is. It was sitting at a table in the store that we grew up in where I finally realized how appreciative I was for Joan being fair with the distribution of funds and property, and I told her so. It was a big job for anyone. We became closer after that talk. She died at the age of 61 from lung cancer while I was incubating pancreatic cancer. I did not find out my diagnosis until two months after she passed.

I am grateful that Joan and Aunt Agnes did a six-generation gene-alogy on my father's side of the family which reference I am using. I wish that I had knowledge about my mother's family, but informa-tion was sketchy.

Two years after they married, my parents bought a country general store (like Ike Godsey's in *The Waltons*). They had owned a nightclub before that time. The store was in central Texas, across Highway 95, from our house built with stones on the exterior. It was my childhood home until I left for college. The store was nearby.

The work was hard, with long hours, for our family members. I did jobs involved in running the store—pumping gas; selling groceries and other merchandise; sweeping concrete floors (with damp sawdust to cut the dust); cleaning the fresh-cut meat counter; serving bar-b-q; racking the balls for those persons playing the game of pool in an adjoining room; washing dishes in a makeshift kitchen; weighing trucks filled with maize sold to our granary and balancing the checkbook for the family business when I was in high school. I was too young to sell beer and liquor from another adjoining area. When I worked in the store, I would, using a small box with a light bulb, "candle" eggs from farmers to make certain the eggs were not cracked or late-stage fertilized. Air conditioning was non-existent in those early days. Can you picture doing hot yoga? I have heard that what does not kill you makes you stronger.

My brother and his wife Betty bought the store from Mother and Daddy in 1972. It was sold in 2012. It was a family business, having been in our family for seventy years. Jim died in 1996 at the age of 50. Betty and their sons ran the store for sixteen years. Betty is a hard-working lively person, full of laughter. She was good for Jim.

Some people cope with life by smoking; drinking; doing drugs; eating; shopping; sex and other addictions. The ways in which Jim and our father chose to cope did not maintain their health.

I don't have fond memories of my father. For many years, while I was in college and beyond, I did not think of him. It was too painful. I always was a dutiful daughter, sending him cards on his birthday; addressing letters to Mother and Daddy; and remembering their anniversary each year. He controlled members of the family, was cruel and physically (not sexually) abusive. I choose not to include further explanation.

For years, when I did think of him, I made excuses for his treatment of my family. I rationalized what his childhood must have been like. His father was a farmer and rancher. Daddy was the second child of four boys and three girls. All but the youngest sister have passed. Daddy was twelve when his mother died. My aunt was six months old (she said yesterday when I telephoned her to ask what my father was like as a boy.) She said all the boys were great; they worked hard. I could tell that she did not want to talk about those times.

The senior Joe remarried, soon after his spouse died, a woman nineteen years his junior, two years older than the oldest boy who was fourteen. They had five children whom I didn't get to know—many children, little money. Fourteen persons were in the household. It takes many hands to do chores on a farm. I saw Daddy's father a few times--never really knew him, my father's mother or step-mother.

It was in the early 2000's when I had grown sufficient agape love that I was able to forgive my father. I remember sitting at my computer writing a letter to him crying, screaming, perhaps using a few curse words--letting out the pent-up feelings accumulated over the years. I was able to forgive my father who had died in 1981 at the age of 67 from a heart attack. I pounded out two pages of ranting but ended by saying that I had grown enough love for us both to forgive him. I crumpled up the pages and set fire to them in the plastic wastepaper basket in the master bath. I had to laugh when the fire melted the plastic to be a lop-sided "pitcher" spout. The purge was worth buying a new, blue wastepaper basket. I think of my father now with compassion. He did the best he could with the life he had as a youngster when values are formed. His role models were lacking, coping with their own wounds. He never told me he loved me, and probably never heard those words himself from his parents. How can anyone pass on what they do not know?

After watching a television Christmas special today, I began remembering Christmases, or rather lack of Christmas celebration, in my family's household. I don't remember decorations or gifts under a tree. I remember in high school, perhaps my senior year, that I received a check in an envelope for working in the store. My parents could take "the gift" off their taxes for an employee. The check was for $600. I used it for college expense. I worked while in college and paid additional loan debt for 10 years after graduating.

I also remember going out to a restaurant on Christmas Day and not having a home-cooked meal. Mother worked all the time and wanted to go out on Christmas when the store was closed. I cannot say that I blamed her.

My childhood was not a happy one, but neither are those of so many. It was what I knew, so it seemed normal.

2.
Jr. High and High School

I spent six years in a Catholic elementary school being filled with religious education by nuns, some of them just out of high school. I attended Mass at the nearby parish church regularly during the school week, and, of course, every Sunday with my parents. I have Catholic knees to prove kneeling on hard, wooden pews. I prayed the rosary and the Stations of the Cross, being duly joyful, sorrowful and glorious as the mystery prescribed. The priest interpreted the Bible for the congregation, mostly about a God to be appeased because we were sinners. I had to make up sins if I could not think of any during the weekly confession. One of the sins was I had poured ketchup on my brother. I still am not sure if that was a mortal or venial sin. In addition, I had told a lie (oh well, fodder for next week's confession.) I was given several Our Fathers and Hail Marys to say for a penance, and admonished not to sin again.

When it was time to be in seventh grade, I followed one of my friends to the public school, that den of iniquity. I felt out of place and went back to the Catholic school after the year was complete. It would be a more sheltered place for me with smaller class sizes and students and teachers who knew each other.

It is while in seventh grade that a terrifying thing happened to me. I started to bleed. It frightened me. It was then that a mature class-mate, daughter of the police chief, told me it was ok; I was becoming a woman. When I asked Mother about it, I remember her saying, "Don't let a boy get in your pants,"--so much for a talk about the birds and the bees. Fortunately, the gym teacher showed a film to the girls and boys, separately, about growing up. Gosh, was I relieved that I was not going to die because of the bleeding.

Being in high school was a busy, popular time for me. I did not have many overnights with girl friends because I had duties in the store and no driver's license until I was past sixteen. The car was not something I could borrow often.

This week, as I looked over the yearbooks I had saved, memories came back to me of our class who had spent years together at St. Mary's School.

Senior year was memorable for me. The booklet of which I was editor (it was decided we would not have a formal yearbook that year) showed that I was involved in fourteen organizations, some of them for more than one year and several in which I had been an officer. In the three years in Library Club, I had been President twice. I did not know at the time that this would become my chosen career. Perhaps the highest honor for me was being chosen Miss SMS by the entire student body. People liked me.

In the graduating class, there were twenty-two of us originally. At the class's 50th reunion, there were seventeen of us left. Five had made their transitions. I attended that reunion in Texas dressed in a slinky red dress; red high-heeled shoes; pearls and matching earrings; highlighted hair; professionally done nails; and forty pounds lighter than my previous weight. The weight had been lost with a recent bout with pancreatic cancer and subsequent chemo. Fortunately, Gemzar and other drugs did not cause hair loss, only thinning of the hair. I looked hot!

Two of my good friends and I sat at the same table with my first "love" Freddy, former captain of every sport played in school. (His wife was there, too.) Freddy picked up the tab for our table at the end of the meal. The organizing committee of the reunion had decided to have music. I was not one to sit still. I picked up a football jacket one of the classmates had brought and placed on a table. I began swinging it over my head and dancing to the music. I had only one-half glass of Corona Lite all night, so I was not inebriated. It was a fun evening, I thought this week as I read Freddy's two pages in my junior yearbook that ended with "I will always love you. P.S. Do not erase."

Freddy's and my relationship was an innocent one. He was the first boy I dated and kissed, after my sixteenth birthday (Daddy's rule); besides, my father owned a shotgun.

Freddy owned a 1956 black and white Ford. He would take me to his at-home football games and bring me home. It seems the second we drove into my driveway, my father would start turning the outside spotlight off and on. I think it meant I had better get in the house yesterday.

It was in my junior and high school years that my father bought a ranch in Burnet, central Texas. Burnet is about an hour east of Taylor. He had cattle and horses on the ranch, and brought Lady and Thundercloud to the barn in our backyard. Although I do not remember a special toy, doll or pet growing up, I remember those horses. I would ride one or the other to an older neighbor girl's house. Evelyn had a horse, too, and lived about a mile away.

It was fun making the horses gallop. Trotting them was a bumpy ride. I rode western style and never had riding lessons. I had dreams of being in the competitive barrel races in the town rodeo each year, but I didn't own a fast quarter horse. Lady was a spirited paint, and Thundercloud was a short pony.

One day when I was riding Lady in the barn area, she almost got me cut in half in my stomach area. She must have been spoofed because she took off like a bolt of lightning and ran under a string of barbed wire between two posts. It was not my time to join the angels, for the girth on the saddle broke, and I fell off. I have also fallen off a horse when I was riding bare back, without a saddle, up a hill.

There are good memories from this time in my life, and I am grateful for them.

I now realize unconscious, latent memories exist from my childhood, and they are coming to light. I was a teen who made good grades in school; worked physically hard; was drug free (although I did experiment with smoking until my brother and I, hiding in an over-turned outhouse behind the store, started a grass fire and were found out); and did everything I could to be worthy of my father's love and approval which never materialized, through no fault of my own.

That revelation, of yearning for a father's love, hit me between the eyes like a cosmic 2x4 when I saw the movie "*Saving Mr. Banks,*" a few days after it was released in late December, 2013. It made a profound impact upon me.

The movie is a "true" story which chronicles, over a period of 20+ years, the negotiations between Walt Disney and P. L. Travers, the author of the Mary Poppins books, for the author's rights to be assigned to Disney to make a movie, which he promised his daughters, lovers of the series, that he would do.

Travers (actually not her real name; she was born Helen Goff) was adamant that there would be no animation or color red, among other stipulations, when she agreed to turn over the rights (due to her dire financial situation). Emma Thompson, who should be an Oscar nominee for best actress, plays Travers. And who does not like Tom Hanks, who has the Disney role?

It is interesting that Pamela insists on being called, "Mrs. Travers." There is no evidence that she ever married. Travers was the first name of her father, played by Colin Farrell, during the movie flashbacks to Helen's childhood in Australia.

I did research after seeing the film. The symbolism in it is evident and poignant. Helen's father died of influenza when she was seven years old. (I have never heard of someone spouting blood when dying from the flu. That symptom would be more likely due to consumption (tuberculosis). Hollywood makes its own rules. The red blood would explain why Travers insisted there be no red in the movie; it reminded her of her father's demise.

The name "Banks" in the books/movie is no accident. In the books, Mr. Banks, a rich banker is uninvolved with his children until he begins singing the song "Let's go fly a kite" and dances outside with kids in tow. He becomes "saved."

But little Helen could not save her father, who had lost his bank job, descended into alcoholism, and died. The family was destitute and moved by train to the last stop on the rail line.

It is a matter of self-preservation when living becomes unbearable that imagination sparks and fantasy steps in to ameliorate the pain. Thus, out of the tragedy of her life, Travers birthed the Mary Poppins masterpieces while attempting to escape reality.

Travers and her father shared an incredible love for one another. During a flashback in the movie and seeing them on horseback, facing one another, with her father holding her tightly, with the sun at her back, brought tears to my eyes. I yearned for a love like theirs.

I am an empath. I was crying with Travers as she watched the movie premiere, to which she was not invited by Disney, but attended anyway. Her sadness was palpable because she could not save her beloved father, the real life Mr. Banks.

Although it was painful for me, I am glad I saw the film. Perhaps the feelings it called forth, and engendered in my soul, will help me to heal.

3.
College Days

After high school graduation, I needed to head off to college to escape working my life away and doing homework after the store closed at 9:00 P.M. Mother and I visited two Catholic colleges in San Antonio taught by the Sisters of Divine Providence and the Sisters of Charity of the Incarnate Word. I chose the former college, Our Lady of the Lake. Patsy, my best friend in high school, decided to go, too. Patsy had been the valedictorian of our senior class, so she got a break on tuition.

Patsy, a-late-in-life child, was the aunt of Freddy, whom you have met in the previous chapter. After the end of the first semester freshman year, Patsy decided to go back home to marry the man she had been dating. We were female friends double-dating male friends our senior year in high school. I made new friends that first year in college and in the years to follow.

Our Lady of the Lake (OLLC) was founded in 1895, and remains with the Divine Providence order of nuns. It is now OLL University and "...offers Bachelor's degrees in 33 areas of study; Master's degrees in 14 areas of study; and two doctoral degree programs." Its statement of purpose is that it "...exists for the purpose of providing undergraduate and graduate programs that are rooted in the tradition of Catholic higher education...." According to the school's history on the Internet, the Main building was destroyed by a four-alarm fire on May 6, 2008. The destruction of the roof, a collapsed spire, and extensive water damage shut down the building for reconstruction until classes were resumed there in January, 2011.

The campus was beautiful with its Gothic architecture—spires, vaulted ceilings, arches, and flying buttresses to hold up the high stone walls. There were trees surrounding Elmendorf Lake on the main campus. Across the street was a new dormitory for freshmen. It was named Pacelli Hall for Eugenio Pacelli, Pope Pius XII, who served from 1939 until his death in 1958.

In Pacelli, there were suites of two girls to a room, sharing a Jack and Jill bathroom. There was a sink in each room. I was lucky to have Ann, a tall, humorous blonde, for my roommate. We were both neat freaks.

I was not so lucky the next year when I became an upperclassman and was able to have a private room with shared bathroom. Sheila-the-Mouth was from Panama and claimed that necessary room with strewing toiletries and clothes throughout. Was it because she had a maid, literally, when she was living in her parents' home? If I wanted a sanitary toilet or tub, I had to clean the porcelain.

I was active in several organizations, including teaching catechism to children on an air force base after mass on Sunday mornings. I concentrated on my studies and dated infrequently, and never seriously.

During a Christmas pageant on the steps in the Main rotunda, I played the part of St. Joseph. The beard was a fake. As the pageant proceeded, I fainted, visibly, in front of the crowd. I was embarrassed. How could I take care of Mary and the Child if I faint because of a lack of fresh air?

It was not until my junior year that I decided upon a major in Library Science after completing enough hours for minors in religion and philosophy—many hours were required in these courses. It was petite, dear Mrs. Emigh, who taught Children's Literature, who made me realize that I wanted to bring children and books together as a career. When she called the roll, instead of responding "here", we had to answer with a nursery rhyme. Her smile was infectious.

I had experienced enough indoctrination over the years that early in my junior year, I felt drawn to join the convent and complete the remainder of my education. When I attended a religious retreat, while in confession, a priest told me if I did not decide now, I would lose my calling. He was right; joining a convent was not meant for this livewire. I was not meant to wear a nun's habit of a one piece, long black dress with sleeves; a black headpiece; a white wimple covering my head, neck, and chin; and a large rosary for praying anytime. I was not destined to be a bride of Christ.

Although OLLC was chiefly an all girls' school, there were a few male day students who did not live on campus. There were allowances for a social life with dances when the local air force officer trainees and a neighboring boys' college were invited. If someone was dating an OT, she would invite a couple of her friends to meet his male friends. Such was the case when I met Pat, my husband-to-be and the father of my children. He was a recent graduate of St. Michael's College in Winooski, Vermont; he kissed my hand when we met. He had a college degree and was a big, smart, hairy man—my kind of guy—and a Catholic to boot. He would soon be an Air Force second lieutenant. We dated for 10 months and married in my senior year at OLLC. It was later that he admitted to me that he initially had his eye on Molly-of-the-Big-Tatas, the classmate who had invited me and another girl to the officers' club of the man she was dating.

Pat was my first experience with Eros, romantic love. He was like no one I had met in my young life. He was experienced in the ways of the world, a contrast to my sheltered self--an almost twenty-one-year-old virgin. He was ambitious and self-assured, and of Irish/English descent. He had red hair and freckles, like the boy in Norman Rockwell's paintings. I fell hopelessly in lust, and he professed his love for me. I was touched when he did the traditional "asking my father for my hand in marriage." The rest of me went with "the hand."

Pat's parents lived in his home town, Rouses Point, New York. My parents in Texas finally accepted that I was going to marry "a Yankee." The wedding was a large community affair in Taylor, Texas, where I was born. My parents had been in business for so long a time that they invited 300 of their closest friends, relatives and business associates. I knew only some of the people who attended. Pat's parents, siblings, and three military groomsmen were the persons he knew who attended. Townspeople looked the Yankee over; some may have decided he was a normal person. There was no "bride's side or groom's side" of the church. The wedding Mass was performed by the church priest. The reception was held at the local Veterans of Foreign Wars (VFW) hall, consisted of a large meal for guests, and an orchestra for dancing.

As I look at the group photo of our wedding, I remember it as a celebration with the groomsmen in military dress--bowties, black jackets and trousers; the groom wore a white jacket, bowtie and black trousers. My sister Joan was the Maid of Honor; my college friend Faye, my high school friend Patsy, and Pat's sister Judy (Dude) were bridesmaids; my cousin Margo was a junior bridesmaid; my cousin Cindy and a youngster I do not recognize were flower girls; and a male youngster was the ring bearer. The bridesmaids looked elegant with dark green velvet tops, empire-waisted, white brocade long skirts, and a green velvet hat with a white short veil. They carried a single white gladiola flower.

I detail the description above because the marriage was a special day; I thought it would last a lifetime. Pat was my "forever" man.

The honeymoon was brief, only a few days. We left for Waco, with the top of Pat's MG convertible sports car down, in the cold of January. But, remember, we were in Texas. Waco was where Pat was stationed. He returned to work, and I returned to college in San Antonio to finish a Bachelor of Arts degree with a major in library science.

4.
Young Married Life

After Waco, we began life in Sacramento, California, the first move of nine in eleven years in the military. Daughter Donna was born in Sacramento. After Pat's additional training near San Francisco, the next assignment was Amarillo, Texas. He was a member of the Strategic Air Command (SAC) and, trained as a navigator for B52 aircraft, had to be on alert (away from home) for several days a week. It was a taste, for me, of what military life would be—frequent moves and additional responsibilities.

Daughter Rhonda was born in Amarillo, Texas, eighteen months after her sister Donna was born. When Rhonda was six weeks old, her father got orders to report to Southeast Asia (Udorn, Thailand) to fight in the Vietnam War. Our family was separated for his tour of one year.

Dad, Pat's father, came to Amarillo to pick up the girls, me, and our Ford Mustang to live in Rouses Point, New York, 40 miles south of Montreal, Canada. We lived with Pat's parents, Mom and Dad. It was a blessing to be with them in what was a stressful time for me with two babies to care for. Had I remained in Amarillo, there was no one to ask for help.

After Pat returned to the states, he got a prized assignment to Minot, North Dakota. North Dakota—where the state tree is a telephone pole and there is one highway which runs north and south amid snowmobile trails. Snow flies horizontally during blizzards. We lived in base housing, with the town of Minot being ten miles away.

I worked as Adult Services Librarian of Minot Public Library for a year. I had a radio program spotlighting library services; edited a monthly library bulletin; and conducted tours for community groups, among other duties. There were few days off from work since the only highway into the town needed to be freed of snow.

The trip from New York to Minot was memorable. We pulled a small camper trailer behind the car and slept in the confined quarters. It was cold, and guess who had to get out from under the warm covers to start the heater in the morning? You are right.

One night the four of us were awakened in the early morning hours when Rhonda rolled out of the top bunk of the camper, smack on top of Pat and me. We were sleeping in the bottom bunk. There was screaming and kicking, mostly by Pat, who must have been back in his war days when attack was imminent. He never wanted to talk about his experiences during that tour.

I also remember Pat coming home, when we were in Minot, with two Siamese kittens inside his flight jacket. The girls squealed with joy. We named the cats Pounce and Bounce, for that is what they did. Guess who had to feed and clean up after the cats? You are right.

I cannot pin-point the assignment when Wolf, (who grew to be a 100 lb. plus German shepherd) was brought home. I remember the kitchen in the house was small. The grown boy had spread his HO gauge model trains and tracks to operate on the kitchen floor. I was trying to make dinner. The behemoth dog raced through, scattering the rail yard. I can still hear Pat's laughter amid the reigning chaos.

The next assignment was Norton AFB in San Bernardino, California, about 60 miles west of Los Angeles. Smog drifted into the valley from LA. The rubber bulb of my turkey baster cracked, as did the hoses under the car's hood, from the pollution. My lungs, and those of my children, had the beginnings of coal miner's disease.

It was the time of Charles Manson and the Tate-LaBianca murders in 1969. Manson was not convicted until January 25, 1971.

The girls had a babysitter when I worked in the San Bernardino Public Library for the year we lived there. Pat still had a schedule of being on alert for several days during a week.

One evening the lights went out in the house. I looked up and down the street to see if others' lights were out. They were. However, my concern did not lessen. Anyone who might have been watching the house knew that a woman and two children lived there, often alone. The next day I went out and bought locks for the back gate and for the outdoor electrical box. Prosecuting attorney in the Manson trial, Vincent Bugliosi, did not write *Helter Skelter: The True Story of the Manson Murders* (W. W. Norton: 1994) until 1994. I did read the book when it came out. I did not know how scared I could have been with the lights going out that night with that madman and his "family" on the loose.

We spent a brief time at Lowery AFB in Aurora, Colorado, where Pat received additional training. I remember our renting a new home (the lawn was not established) and spending Christmas Day in the house with no furniture. The furniture was to be delivered after Christmas. We had a tree with a few scraggly decorations and celebrated the best we could.

The last military assignment was in Plattsburgh, New York, about 25 miles south of Pat's hometown of Rouses Point, on the Canadian border, and across Lake Champlain from Burlington, Vermont. All the moving hassle was over (I thought).

It was good to be in a town/village of 2,500 persons with Pat's family surrounding us. It seemed that everyone knew everyone else's business, something to which I was not accustomed. But I adjusted because there were so many positives in living there.

Geographically, it is beautiful, with the Green Mountains of Vermont nearby. We lived in a small, white Cape Cod style, older home with two big picture windows in front overlooking Maple Street (read vibrant, colorful leaves in the fall). There were two white, long-necked, ceramic egrets facing each other in the right window near the fireplace. The windows in the living/dining room had celery green sheers to give the area softness. I put Pergo in the entryway with a place for boots and a closet for coats. The carpet was beige, but in good shape. The kitchen was not ideal with red indoor-outdoor carpeting and outdated metal cabinetry. I gave it a bit of a modern look with orange, white and silver geometric wallpaper above the cabinets; it was an eat-in kitchen and had three windows. There was a small bedroom (rail yard) and half bath downstairs. Upstairs there was a full bath and two large bedrooms. The girls shared one bedroom with white gilded, matching furniture from Sears. There was a nook in our bedroom where I set up my make-up vanity purchased at an auction in Alburg, Vermont, across the lake. One of my friends and I would often go to the auction house where you could even buy live chickens if you wanted.

It was later that we had the basement finished and divided into various areas like a closet lined with real cedar wood and an office area with a large wooden desk. These areas were on either side of the stairs. There was a large family room with a wood-burning Ben Franklin stove with a couch facing the stove. The enclosed area behind the family room contained the washer, clothes dryer, furnace, and a sump pump in the event of water seepage.

In front of the 271' backyard, one block from Lake Champlain, was a detached garage at the end of a long, snow-gathering drive-way. I mowed the grass of that massive backyard in the summer and shoveled snow from that long driveway extending to the street in the winter—just in time to have the town's snowplow deposit a hill of snow in the driveway entrance which was too high to drive the car over it when I had to go to work in a nearby town.

The girls had a safe, pretty neighborhood, across from their elementary school in which to grow up. They were treated like princesses by the family, so says their mother, the Queen. When we moved there, Donna was in first grade, and Rhonda was in kindergar-ten. I walked across the street from the house to work as the school's Library Media Specialist three days a week and drove, two days a week, to a town 5 miles away to supervise the school library there. In the school library across from the house, the anteroom was the former nurse's office, a bit tight for instructing classes of 20+ students and checking out books to the little readers. A small, former class-room, library adjoined the anteroom.

I worked in the district for seven years; dispersed an intermediate (grades 4-6) collection into two existing primary libraries when that library became a junior high school library. I served as the librarian there. Jane, the high school librarian, was a few hallways away in an adjoining building. In addition to meeting classes on a weekly basis, I helped formulate a Materials Selection policy for the district. My subsequent employment will be summarized in the Career and Rewards chapter.

We saw Pat's parents and extended family often. It was by being surrounded by his family members that I first began to experience love expressed—hugs and joyous words. I felt that family members, when they asked, "How are you?", they really wanted to know, that they cared. It was Philos (brotherly, family), bordering on Agape, love. I was coming closer to the top of the love ladder.

In the late 1970's, Pat was elected Mayor of his hometown. I did not realize how much I did in the role of First Lady to welcome new-comers until I recently attended the wedding in New York of the son of my long-time friend, Donna. We have stayed in touch, particularly with Christmas letters, over the years. I had attended her son Roger's baptism; he is now 34 and married. Also at the wedding was Donna's and my friend Faye.

I asked Donna if she remembered how we met. She said it was when Pat was mayor, and I gave a coffee in my home and invited the newcomer ladies in town. I even invited ladies of the political oppo-sition. Faye said that we met when I gave her a call and invited her to tour a historic home in Plattsburgh. She had two young boys and no babysitter. I called Kathy, the teen who took care of my girls on occasion. Faye then had a sitter, and off we went. I had not seen Faye since I left Rouses Point in 1981. Donna and I had gotten together a few years ago when I had gone back to Rouses Point to see my daugh-ter Donna who lived in the area at the time. My friend and I went to Stowe, Vermont and had coffee at the von Trapp home (think The Sound of Music movie) which was open to the public.

It was great re-living old times with the two friends. I must share a story of dancing at the wedding. Donna, her husband Cliff, Faye and I were dancing as a group. Donna and Faye sat down after a time, so it was Cliff and me on the floor. We then started dancing with others to The Twist. I was dancing with a young man, probably in his 30's. I asked him to be careful because I am old. He said, "What, 37?" I said, "Double it!" Dancing did wonders for my spirit; not so for my sore hip.

Politics in Rouses Point was not a picnic. My daughters were taunted at school for their father's stand on local issues. I remember one day in particular when the town judge's (opposing party) son was peering into the kitchen windows of our house scaring the girls who began screaming. Pat was somewhere in the town, unavailable. I telephoned Mark, whom I considered a friend, and who had been Pat's campaign manager. He came right over and chased the little varmint away.

Pat told me he was going to resign as mayor; he said I was too weak to handle his continuing in office. Hairs stood up on the back of my neck and a first glimmer of Self-Love asserted itself. I told him it was HIS decision to resign, and that I did not accept responsibility for blame.

No one can make you feel inferior without your consent.
Eleanor Roosevelt

Pat did some of the meal preparation when he was out of work after the military. All other responsibilities were mine while holding a full-time job. I began to realize that I had married a Peter Pan Man, one who never seemed to grow up and accept responsibility in a marriage.

The state required their librarians to hold classroom teaching certificates in addition to library certifications. I attended the University of Vermont (about 60 miles away) during summers to satisfy the twelve semester hours of education courses required. I took the courses on a graduate credit level. I knew I would get a Master's degree in Library Science rather than 30 additional hours after a

Bachelor's degree. I could transfer a portion of these hours toward the post-graduate degree.

I registered to attend the University of New York at Albany, a three-hour drive from Rouses Point. I stayed on campus during the week and drove home on weekends to be with the girls and complete household chores. I received a M.L.S. degree in the summer of 1979.

In the fall of 1980, events began falling into place which led to my decision to leave the marriage. It is said that when it becomes too painful to remain in a situation, change is inevitable.

Pat had been working in Burlington where, and I agree, the distance of 60 miles one way was too far to drive each day particularly during the winter months. So he got an apartment there and came home weekends to have his laundry done. When he was transferred to Plattsburgh with the company, he chose to rent another apartment even though the 25-mile distance was drivable on the I-87 Thruway which was kept clear of snow. He chose not to have a phone. I was married, living life as a single parent. His financial contribution to the family lessened with his expenses of rent, utilities and restaurant meals.

I remember this sequence of events clearly. I was outdoors, on a ladder, lifting a heavy, glass and wood storm window to hook onto a kitchen window. It was cold. Pat was at the camp, hunting.

The next scenario was that I had taken the girls shopping in Plattsburgh for winter coats. We stopped by their father's apartment to show him our purchase. I could hear a child's voice inside. I knocked several times before he answered the door, disheveled--no socks in his shoes; his hair uncombed; and his shirt unbuttoned. That weekend at home, I asked him if he was having an affair; his answer, predictably, was "No; I was watching a football game."

It must have been in June the next year when, as I was crying into the dishwater surrounding my hands, that I decided I was leaving and taking the girls with me to Texas. My father had died on May 26, and I did not know how Mother would be after being married for 40 years and now alone. I wanted to be in a city, so I began searching for a job in Houston, not that I knew anyone there. It was after I made the decision to leave that one of my friends, who worked in Plattsburgh, said that she had seen Pat in town with several different women. Granted, they may have been clients.

There was an opening for a librarian in Houston I.S.D., an urban district. I sent for, and filled out, the application paperwork. I also telephoned the principal of the school expressing my interest (site, literally, unseen). That telephone call got me the job, and she recommended me to the human resources department. I began preparations to move in July.

It was also in July, prior to my leaving, that Pat's father had a heart attack and was in the hospital. Since Pat could not be reached by telephone, his sister had to go to his door with the news. There was sadness in my leaving. I loved his parents and other relatives.

Gone were the days of having Dad coming over to make repairs in the house. Pat's younger brother is a lot like Dad was. He was handy, and clearly a family man. I loved Terry and his wife Peggy. I told them afterward that the most difficult part of the divorce was losing them as family.

My decision brought difficulty for my elder daughter Donna. She said, just the other day, that, at the age of sixteen, she had two weeks to make a decision whether to go to Texas or remain with her father. She loved us both. She chose to remain with her father. It was a good choice for him. She graduated from Plattsburgh High School. Rhonda came with me; her relationship with her father remains rocky. Rhonda had adjustments her freshman year in high school. We lived in an apartment in Houston a block from her school. Many of the kids in Spring Branch High School came from affluent homes, which situation was difficult for her. In spite of it all, I knew I had made a wise decision.

Forever was ending, but not before an emotionally painful four years.

5.
Second Chance for Love

As I mentioned in the former chapter, I accepted the job as Library Media Specialist of Eliot Elementary School in the Houston Independent School District. The school was located across the city in the east part of town, just north of I-10, Katy Freeway (more aptly called "parking" lot). With all the traffic, it took 30 minutes to drive a distance of 4 miles to the loop. I still had a long way to drive.

I adored my principal, an elegant Hispanic lady who had a doctorate degree to manage one of the four largest elementary schools in the district—1,200 students. Some days, I had 10 classes of students in addition to day-to-day upkeep and getting books back on the shelves.

I believe the former librarian was born in the school nurse's office and grew to be a disorganized lady in her job. I am not even sure that she liked children. To keep them from "messing up" the popular dinosaur and joke books, the books were housed behind her desk, out of Dewey Decimal sequence. When I looked under the sink in the tiny workroom, there were stacks of catalog cards (before electronic catalogs) about 2 feet high. I did not know if the cards belonged to new books that had not been filed into the wooden catalog drawers, of if they belonged to books which had been withdrawn from the collection. I never did find out their status.

I applied for and won a $3,000 Exxon funded grant to update the reference collection (when encyclopedias were still in print form); buy a typewriter (no computers in the early 1980's); and for the Library Director of the district, also a supportive person, to pay someone over the summer to sort and make sense of the aforementioned card stacks.

I put in bright yellow signage on the shelves so that the students could locate different sections of the library. I taught library reference skills and read stories to the younger children. Book fairs were held for those students wishing to buy books. Eliot was not in an affluent neighborhood, but parents, chiefly of Hispanic heritage, wanted their children to read and become proficient in the English language.

There were no library assistants or parent volunteers. This library needed me, and I needed it to fill more than my hours at work. I began to make my own "help." I had the co-operation of the teachers to lighten my load. I filed the check-out cards according to teacher classes. The day before the class's library day, I would put the cards in the teacher's mail box for the older students, who could read, to put the correct card in each of their two books. The teachers put the cards in the books for the kindergarten and first grade students.

After the place was finally in order, I taught the older students to shelve their own books to the third number in the Dewey system (so all dog books, e.g., would be together). I did not worry about the numbers after the decimal point. They also shelved their fiction books according to the first three letters of the author's last name. The younger students placed their books on the well-identified single letter of the author's last name on the Easy section shelves.

After two years of driving/sitting in traffic congestion, I applied for a job in a suburban district closer to my home that was situated on the west side, where traffic was not the problem it was in going across the city. My time at Eliot was becoming complete.

When I said I needed a job to fill my time outside of the workday, I often took paperwork home to keep busy. I was in deep mourning for the loss of the dream which should have been-- being married to a charming prince, with two lovely children, living in a Cape Cod-style home. But that was not to be. I never regretted the decision to leave, but was heart-break lonely for four years. I had left close friends behind. I did not try to date. I was still married and honored those vows made almost seventeen years ago.

When I was ready to let go after three years of being separated, I asked Pat to have his attorney friend draw up the divorce papers. I retained an attorney in Houston to look after my interest. I told Pat he could charge me with abandonment if he needed to state grounds for the dissolution.

I continued to struggle financially. There was no alimony or child support (we each had a daughter living with us). Teaching is not known as a high income profession. After the divorce was finalized, I did receive a few thousand dollars, perhaps not as much as if the house was sold and the proceeds divided. I had put all of my paychecks into maintaining the household in New York. With the long winters and the price of fuel oil, saving was improbable over the years. Pat and his new wife had "made improvements" and continued to live in the house. According to Pat's attorney, the settlement was "fair."

Forever had ended.

It would be another year before I joined "Say Gourmet," a group of singles in Houston who would go out to dinner together.

I remember what I was wearing the night I met Bob. It was a black wool skirt, which I had borrowed from my daughter Rhonda and which I still have and wear; a long-sleeved white crepe blouse; a pearl necklace and earrings; and a full-length, oatmeal-colored wool coat I had received from my mother for Christmas. The date was February 6, 1985.

The setting of the dinner, with 25-30 persons present, was an ornate, elegant Italian opera house restaurant, The Great Caruso. There was live, on-stage entertainment. Bob was in conversation with a wealthy female business owner on his left, and I chatted with the male teacher across the table from me. I was surprised, at the end of the evening, when Bob invited me to meet him for a drink at Vargo's, another first-rate restaurant which had peacocks wandering the lush grounds.

Bob was a Professor of Marketing at the University of Houston and had published three books. He had a D.B.A. (Doctorate of Business Administration), was intelligent, humorous, and, frankly, handsome. He said he liked me because, as a teacher, I had summers off.

When the restaurant bar was closing for the evening, he invited me to a hayride on Saturday that the singles group in his church was sponsoring. I met the group at the appointed place and time. Bob's friend Martha (perhaps they had dated) told Bob that Max could "take care of me" during the hayride. Destiny stepped in.

I was invited to Bob's Methodist church for the following day. The single ladies looked me over. I think I was infringing on their "territory." Bob invited me out to dinner for the following Tuesday. Our first official date was at Carmelo's Italian restaurant on Memorial Drive, near where I lived.

Ariel was the nimble-fingered Russian pianist at the restaurant. Bob undoubtedly had brought other women on dates there. When Ariel saw Bob, and I was introduced, Ariel good-naturedly called Bob "sex fiend." Ariel was an attractive man, and I got nervous standing next to him--so much for my not dating for many years.

Bob and I became "an item" and were married four months later. Our marriage was Eros and Philos love combined. We were friends as well as lovers. Bob was a big brown teddy bear without a bear attitude. We had so much in common—integrity; being extroverts, social creatures, and writers; educated; interested in fine food and entertaining; being neat and punctual. I was to learn from our extensive travels that we were both adventurers. We shared a love of the Colorado Rockies and were building a house in Creede, Colorado, where Bob owned land and where his family (wife and four sons) had spent summers while camping. Sue, Bob's wife of 20+ years, had passed from cancer two years before we met.

When we had dated about three months and were out dancing, Bob asked me what I would say if he asked me to marry him. I told him I would think about it (after the lost of trust in the first marriage).

In the intervening days before we met again, I made a list of pros and cons to make a decision. There were many pros on my list. The only cons I wrote were the age difference (he was 16 years my senior); that he seemed ultra religious; and that he didn't like eggplant. The last con hardly qualified as important.

On our next date, I told him my answer was "yes." He reminded me he said "If." He quizzed whether I had dental bills coming up or credit card bills. I felt like he was treating me like a horse he might be interested in buying although he did not have me open my mouth to check my teeth. I backed away emotionally. He sensed my becoming distant.

After some time, he said I should ask him when I was ready. So I did. With my characteristic sense of humor, I planned the scenario. We were in his apartment after church one Sunday. I asked him to find music on the radio. He tuned into a baseball game, not acceptable. I had brought my basket for the proposal. I lit the candles I had brought. I got down on one knee and handed him a wide-lined tablet sheet (like the one first graders use when they begin writing their alphabet) and a crayon. On the paper I had printed, "I love you. Will you marry me?' Below those words were boxes labeled "yes" or "no." He hesitated to develop suspense. He then put an "x" in "yes" box. I handed him a live rose and put a paper ring, taken from a cigar I had purchased, on his left hand. In the event he marked "no", I had a scallion onion ready to present. We celebrated over a bottle of Asti Spumante.

We had an active social life with friends in the singles group in the Methodist Church Bob had been attending. Although I had lived my life as a Catholic, after about a year I became a Methodist. I knew many people in that church, and I liked the Methodist focus on social action. I never felt there to be exclusion in that church.

After we married and our leases were up on our respective apartments, we bought a townhouse and joined a larger Methodist church (with 6,000 members) near the home we had purchased. The house was not far from my third school in Houston, the one for which I had won a number of grants. The house was closer to my job than it would have been had I stayed in the suburban district. I discovered a route to work which enabled me to by-pass traffic on the congested freeway. Rhonda had graduated in 1985 and was in college in central Texas.

Bob and I worked at our respective jobs during the school year, and traveled during the summer, holidays, and spring break. We were D.I.N.K.s (double income, no kids) and traveled the world, soaking up different cultures, and meeting people. It was a grand, happy life for twelve years. Summers spent in the mountains of Colorado were a refreshing break from the high humidity and heat of Houston.

When we moved permanently to Colorado Springs, we bought our dream home. It was where we planned to spend the remainder of our lives. The subdivision was in the northern, newer part of the city, south of the Air Force Academy. The house had four levels, perfect for all the entertaining we would do. It had a double-car garage. The first floor contained the living room, a dining area, and the kitchen. One floor lower was the family room, stereo, fireplace and television. We finished off the lowest level (basement) ourselves which consisted of a study area, small television, a bedroom with twin beds, and a bath with a double-wide Jacuzzi tub. The topmost level had a master bedroom, laundry (convenient to have the washer and dryer upstairs); master bath; a full bath near Bob's office; and a guest bedroom.

I never had reason to question Bob's faithfulness in the years we were married. Our personalities and interests were similar, and we had fun in our marriage. It was a happy time for each of us.

A short time after we moved to Colorado Springs, we saw an ad in the newspaper for those couples over 50 interested in joining a social group in the neighborhood of Briargate, where we lived. Co-incidentally, four of the males were named "Bob." The four Bobs became golfing partners. Elaine's husband, whom I mention in Chapter 8, was a Bob (and probably still is a Bob).

My Bob and I re-lived a childhood together which neither of us had growing up. His father died when Bob was twelve. Although Bob was two years younger than his brother Jack, Bob assumed the role of first-born, the responsible leader. It was time each of us let loose and enjoy silly times. You will see from photos in this book that the brilliant, studious professor was game to dress as Tweedle Dum from "Alice in Wonderland." I was Tweedle Dee. (Dee was the nickname Bob's sons called me.) I must tell you the story of our costumes.

We had been invited to a Halloween party, costumes required. We had the "fat/egg-shaped" description down with no effort. We had green-striped knee socks left over from our Raggedy Ann and Andy costumes. I had ordered two blue bow ties, matching propeller beanies, large rubber ears, and green suspenders from a catalog. The challenge was matching shirts and pants. We went to Wal-Mart (or Target) to the maternity department where we found a solution. The pants were expandable to fit Bob, and retractable to fit me. Bob joked about getting a matching purse to go with his outfit.

Another time, the golfing buddies had a laugh when Bob unzipped his golf bag on the course. Inside was a small teddy bear wearing an "I (heart) Bob" T-shirt.

I would surprise my husband on his birthdays with creative parties like a picnic in a park or a scavenger hunt in the house, with small gifts and notes leading to the next place to look. Once when we were in Creede, along with four of our friends, I wrapped up a red lady's negligee as his gift—ultimately, it was a gift for him when I wore it. Another time, during social time in our Sunday School class, I carried out a Spiderman theme with a cake, napkins, punch and balloons. It was his 69th birthday. I bought giant candles to read "96", 69 reversed. I smile now.

We both enjoyed the birthday hot-air balloon ride over Houston. Early that morning, when Bob got in the car, I had him put on a blindfold. (I drove, naturally.) We arrived at an appointed spot on the outskirts of the city. The pilot made a show of holding a small, un-inflated balloon to test wind direction. When we were airborne, and he saw that we were game, he dipped into a body of water. We almost landed on a fence, but managed to clear it by rocking the balloon. Upon disembarking, we celebrated by getting on our knees, grabbing a small paper cup with champagne in our teeth, and pouring it over our heads while trying a catch a drink of it.

It must be my Leo ascendant in astrology. Leo is creative. I never ran out of ideas for unique celebrations for us. Bob thoroughly enjoyed dinner in a fine restaurant on another birthday. I had arranged for the performing belly dancer to present him with a rose at our table.

Another time, I sent flowers to be delivered to him while he was teaching his university marketing class. His department chair (boss) brought them to him. That man was loved.

Just before my 50th birthday, I mentioned I would like to have a party after all the ones I had planned for him. Bob didn't say anything about making arrangements. On the date of my birth, he said we were picking up Elaine and Bob and going to dinner. Elaine and my Bob had planned a surprise party at Elaine's house and had invited many of our friends. Sometimes, to inspire Bob to be creative, I had to give a nudge like the time I mailed him a brochure of a Valentine's weekend special at a nice hotel on the beach in Galveston with a note saying "Surprise your Valentine." (I think he guessed it was from me.)

With love and laughter those many years, "What happened?" I asked myself. As I mention in Chapter 7, in 1996, I began to consider leaving the marriage. I wanted to go, do, be; Bob was be-ing mostly in front of the television. I was becoming frustrated with the difference in our ages. Perhaps he began slowing down because of his health. He had been diagnosed with diabetes two weeks before our marriage. He was insulin-dependent. Because he was not a complainer, I did not know the toll his health was taking. I know now that I am older, with non-insulin dependent diabetes, the changes that can happen— fatigue, neuropathy, malaise.

Bob had always been a snorer, and I did not sleep well unless I fell asleep before he did. I began sleeping in the bedroom in the basement. It was quieter there. Bob had also begun to pressure me to go back to work to contribute financially. Since Bob had retired, I felt I had also retired after so many years of working. I did not want to work full-time again as a librarian, so I took courses to become a certified nursing assistant and took care of persons part-time in their homes.

The 7-year-old wild child next door, along with the family's constantly barking dog, began to get on my nerves. I had tried talking with the boy's mother about his screaming outdoors, playing on and damaging our lawn. She seemed in another world coping with life with children and "home-schooling" the wild child. Talking with the boy did no good. I like kids. I spent my career surrounded by them. Our house was two blocks down from an elementary school. I counted 30 children on the short street where we lived.

I am an outgoing person. I became withdrawn, spending more time in my woman cave, reading. One of the books that made a life-changing difference was Neale Donald Walsch's *Conversations with God*, Book 1 (G. P. Putnam's Sons: 1995). I am an avid reader, but it took me six months to read this book. I kept picking it up and putting it down. It said that the most important relationship was with yourself, self-love. With my being the giving, nurturing person I am, that concept was difficult for me. It sounded selfish. I came to learn the truth of Neale's words as time went on. I met the man, with his twinkling eyes and sparkling wit, when he spoke at Unity Church in Houston. Book 1 was the first of nine in his "conversations" series. I have twelve of his books on my "favorites" bookshelves. His latest book is *What God Said: The 25 Core Messages of Conversations with God That Will Change Your Life and the World* (Berkley Books: 2013). I particularly like message 1. We are all One, and message 12. Love is all there is. I just purchased the book, and it will be my next read.

I mention in Chapter 9 that I had begun reading books on metaphysical topics in my 30's. In my 50's, I was continuing to do so. Whenever I saw an author-speaking event, or topic with which I was familiar, I attended. It was at a talk on reincarnation where I met my dear friend, Sally. She sat in an empty seat next to me. She said I smiled at her. We began chatting afterward and found we had many interests in common. In retrospect, I know we had a sacred contract to meet and become friends. Sally had been a kindergarten teacher for over 30 years and had/has a gift of psychic counseling. She can read the Akashic records and gives spiritual guidance for clients. We met in 1995, and she returned to her home state of California in

1999, the year I found the library job in February. I could not have gotten through those two horrific years, before I left the marriage, without her friendship and counsel. We have kept in touch over the past 19 years and have visited in person a couple of times. We each have a telephone plan with unlimited calling. Most of our conversations are one to one and one-half hours long. We just pick up where we left off the last time. We are close, like sisters.

I mention in Chapter 7 that I began to consider leaving the marriage in 1996 during the trip to Australia. It was in 1997 during our trip to Greece that I was becoming closer to a decision. In addition to the age and health differences between Bob and me, there were two other serious issues which I choose not to discuss. I had to face the loss of financial security, which was a big concern for this fiscally responsible female. I was not retired with a pension or meager social security income and had not yet found full-time work.

I was energized by the energy of the land of Greece. In Delphi, my toes were vibrating in my sneakers. I mentioned that powerful experience to the guide, Patrick, the man from Dublin, who is mentioned in Chapter 7.

Patrick, as the tour company's representative, picked Bob and me up from the airport in a taxi upon our arrival. The driver took the three of us to the hotel in Athens. I felt a strange attraction to Patrick. We were each married to other persons, and there was no impropriety. Sometime during the trip, the two of us were coming in opposite directions around the corner of a building, nearly colliding. He said to me, "I thought you were going to attack me." My mental response was, "Would you have minded?"

There was chemistry between Patrick and me. The song made popular by Aretha Franklin "(You Make Me Feel Like) A Natural Woman" kept running through my head like an earwig. Early in the trip, I had a vision of Patrick and me as husband and wife living in Greece centuries ago. I could see myself luxuriating in a marble bath with him kissing my neck. There was a blonde, curly-haired toddler, about 2, nearby. The next scene, I saw Patrick as a musician playing the lyre (How did I imagine that ancient instrument and its name?)

I knew (inner knowing) that we had been together in a past life, and my soul recognized the connection.

Our tour group went on a cruise of the Greek Isles. When Bob and I checked into our cabin, there was music playing on the intercom. I wanted to dance; Bob didn't. I cried myself to sleep that night, frustrated with heightened, joyful energy unable to be expressed.

Bob and I were sitting on the beach on one of the islands one evening watching the sunset over the water. Bob was complaining about the cost of the orange juice we were sipping. Where had romance gone?

One evening on the ship, Patrick entertained the group by singing and playing his guitar. (He is a musician in this life, too.) His song was one made popular by Jim Reeves, "He'll Have to Go." (Put your sweet lips a little closer to the phone....) I sat with sandals on my feet, wearing my Grecian dress with gold trim. I was uncomfortable because I felt he was singing directly to me. I felt passion for the man.

Patrick and I did have a few opportunities to be in conversation apart from the group. I asked him if he believed in reincarnation. He did not answer affirmatively but did not dismiss the idea either. Neither of us spoke of our respective marriages, although at one time he did say that he and his wife had grown apart. He talked of his love for Greece, that he and his grandfather spent time there when he was growing up.

We were walking together, with a small group behind us, to some ruins near the countryside resort near where we all were staying. I told Patrick that there was such joy in meeting him again.

The day of the group's departure, people were standing in line saying goodbye to one another. We hugged, and I thanked Patrick for making the trip magical. He kissed me on both cheeks saying, "Greece will see you again." We never had contact again.

In 2000, three years after the trip to Greece, I was on a tour of Ireland with the same company. Since our tour guide was from Dublin and worked for the same company, I asked him if he knew Patrick (no details given) except that he had been the guide in

Greece. The man had seen Patrick just the week before. They had roomed together while leading their respective tours in Ireland.

I did not ask, but he volunteered that Patrick and his wife were divorced. He said she was a lovely lady who spoke several languages.

My decision became apparent the following year. I no longer wanted to spend my life in a marriage where my soul was dying. I wanted to feel alive again. I began to experience self-love. It meant the survival of my spirit.

When Bob and I sat down for a "talk," I told him how I was feeling. He said he thought everything was fine until I "messed" it up. (Actually, he used a more colorful, unprintable term.) He said I had changed. I told him he was right, that I had changed. Since we did not read the same type of books, and we could not discuss our philosophies, he did not know what was happening with me. This butterfly was ready to leave the chrysalis which had grown up around her, suffocating the beautiful creature within.

This penultimate (next to the last) chapter written was the most difficult one to write in the manuscript. It was painful, and I shed many tears while doing so. Although I do not regret my decision, I still love Bob. I send him pink love energy and wish him well. I don't know how or where he is in the years which have intervened. I feel our sacred contract was completed. Just because we no longer live together, the true beauty of love does not cease to exist.

6.
Career and Awards

My career, chiefly as a public school Library Media Specialist, brought creativity, laughter, and learning. I enjoyed working with youngsters of all ages, from kindergarten through high school. Most of the twenty-one years in education were spent in elementary schools. I was required to have an all-level teacher's certificate in addition to librarian certification. After the Bachelor of Arts degree, I went on to earn a Master's degree because a professional position outside of schools required a graduate degree in the subject. I spent time in two public libraries and a summer as a reference librarian in a college library.

The thread of my career picks up during the second school, and new district, in Houston. I had detailed the first one earlier. I spent four years in the new, suburban district, on the west side of the city. I drove against traffic and the commute took a shorter time. The school was being built, had a smaller student body, and needed an energetic librarian who could order new materials, organize various systems, and supervise a library aide (a bonus) and several parent volunteers. Since the builders were finishing up, we set up a work area in the summer in the Junior High library nearby. All processed materials were put into boxes as they were completed. I had the good sense to mark the boxes as Reference, Non-Fiction, Fiction, or Story

Collection bound for different sections in the library. Time was of the essence. The principal wanted the books on the shelves the day school opened. No other library in the district had opened the first day of school. I was relieved no one checked to see if the books were in Dewey order on the shelves. That process was accomplished afterward. The principal was pleased that the Learning Resources Center was "open", and books were on the shelves.

The facility was state-of-the-art. Everything was new. The LRC was in the center of the building. There were audio-visual pods outside of each grade level where classes could gather.

The principal had a flair for decorating. There was a large, semi-circular circulation desk; a carousel with painted horses; a hot air balloon with a square, padded basket in which a couple of children could read; a theater with puppets; three large bulletin boards to decorate, etc. The school had its own Ellison die cut machine with letters and symbols for saving time for teachers doing bulletin boards. I kept 4" block-cut red letters in an alphabetical folder so I did not have to re-make letters each time I changed a display. This media center was a dream every librarian should have at least once in her/his career.

The professional challenge and experience of organizing a new library would serve me well when I returned to Houston several years later and applied for a job in a new charter school library.

I left the above suburban district after four years, and I found myself, for the next four years, in a third district in the Houston area. That school was closer to the townhouse Bob and I had purchased. We had married in 1985 and were to be in the Houston area until 1992. That year Bob retired from the university, and we moved to Colorado Springs.

During those ten years in the Houston area, I excelled in my career, earning many accolades which I will mention later in this chapter.

At one time, I had a small album of photos of reading programs I had initiated and took along to job interviews. I smile as I recall the fun, laughter, and learning that the children and I shared over the years. I know that album still exists somewhere among my belongings, I just did not locate it when I began writing about my career. I am organized and am not a collector of stuff; it will show up.

I relate from memory, in no particular order, some of the reading programs I conducted for various grade levels. Many of them were financed by the competitive grants I won. I believed every child should be a contest winner, not just the super-bright ones who always received honors in many ways.

The first program that comes to mind was *Clifford, the Big Red Dog*. The program was for first and second graders either for them to be read to, or to read the series themselves. When a child was encouraged by a teacher and joined the program, he or she received a genuine dog bone treat to wear. A pin had been glued to the back-side of the bone. The front of the bone displayed the dog treat company's name.

I wrote to the company's CEO, telling him about the free advertising his firm was receiving. Surprisingly, a huge box arrived at the school with lots of toys for cats and dogs, children's pets. Bow Wow!

The Scholastic Company provided a Clifford suit that was available through a company I had used for book fairs. I think it was John, the company's owner, who dressed in the suit at a party culminating the end of the program. The children were delighted.

I love geography. That is how "Read around the World" came into being for intermediate students, grades 3-5. One of the PTA parents, who had artistic talent, designed passports for the participants. Maps with destinations were included in the passport.

The children had a large number of choices of where they wanted to go in the world. Distance in miles was the determining factor in number of books to be read. To keep participants honest, I might ask a couple of questions about the books they were reporting. They were able to choose their modes of transportation (courtesy of the Ellison die cut machine), put their name on the boat, plane, etc. to be displayed on a wall near the school office.

If you are looking for quantities of inexpensive party decorations or incentives, www.orientaltrading.com is a source I used many times.

For this geography program, every child got a globe pencil sharpener for participating, along with other rewards.

Another fun program was "Leap into Learning" which had a frog theme; therefore, frogs and lily pads were on display in the hallway. The PTA president, who was a library volunteer, and her friend created Felicia, the Fancy-Dancing-Frog costume. Felicia, the name chosen by the wearer, put her ballet skills on display and enchanted the children with her moves. I have the photo of her whispering in my ear at the party.

First graders study farms and farm animals. So was born "Reading Eggs-travaganza," a grant winner. Once a week, on Mondays, children would bring in their reading or being-read-to records signed by parents. I think the parameters were 15 minutes for 5 of 7 days. The teacher of the class with the highest percentage of slips turned in got to wear a pair of ridiculously large, felt chicken feet all that week. Paper eggs, displaying the child's name, decorated a wall in the school.

I would occasionally wear the feet myself. It was an open-concept school with perhaps a blackboard sectioning off one class from another. It was like being in a roomful of 500 children and teaching adults. The library was also open concept.

One day as I was wearing the feet on my way to the office, an exasperated fifth grade teacher called out, "Mrs. Eckles, will you please come in for the students to take a look so that we can get back to our lesson." I obliged and may have performed a short version of the popular "chicken dance" you may have seen on the dance floor at weddings.

Another successful program in that school was inspired by Gail Gibbons's book *Sunken Treasure* (Crowell: 1988). Ms. Gibbons has written and illustrated over 130 non-fiction books. The aforementioned book was awarded a place on the Texas Bluebonnet Award list which encourages reading "the best books" for students in grades 3-6. The award was established in 1979.

I don't remember the circumstances which brought Ms. Gibbons to speak at our school, but the reading program built around her title was successful with our intermediate students. They were prepared and knew the books she had written. On the day that she came, we all dressed as pirates. One third grade boy had on an eye patch, a sketched-on-his-face beard, an earring, a handkerchief on his head, a stuffed parrot on his shoulder, and a peg leg. He brought a crutch so that he could stand. His picture is in the "brag" album. Of course, we made a big welcome with bulletin boards and other displays. I had the honor of having Ms. Gibbons stay in my home overnight.

Sunken Treasure is based on the true story of the Atocha, a Spanish galleon (a large sailing ship), which sunk during a hurricane off the cost of Florida in 1622, with treasure aboard. Ms. Gibbons researches each non-fiction topic about which she writes.

As an incentive in the reading program, children were allowed to dig for buried treasure (small marine trinkets) contained in a waist-high rectangular sand box in the library. Beware the varmints who dug without permission. They were forced to walk the plank.

The last program I wish to mention is "Meet the Author." I initiated that program in the first school I served in Houston. The children in the neighborhood were not from affluent families. I dare to say there were few, if any, books in their homes. A book fair, for a chance to buy books, was only mildly successful. So the children became authors themselves. They wrote and submitted their efforts which were spiral-bound and placed on a special shelf in the library for others to check out and read. Each book had a check-out card with the "author's" name and title of the book. Before the program began, we studied the parts of a book during library class.

Now for awards received. I was chosen "Teacher of the Year" by the advisory council in the urban school mentioned. JoAnn, a kindergarten teacher, said among other compliments in my nomination, that "her kids' eyes would light up each time they came into the library. They were always welcomed with a smile, laughter, and a story."

Because I had won an international contest, sponsored by the *Instructor*, a premier teachers' magazine, I was chosen "Teacher of the Year" of the new-school suburban campus. My idea, which I was told was among the 500 entries submitted of using poetry with children, won the Grand Prize and was featured in the April, 1985, issue of *Instructor*. The focus of the program, "Poetry Pockets" was a mannequin in the LRC, who was wearing an apron with multiple, fabric pockets (made by a volunteer) stuffed with poems--original, photocopied, borrowed, whatever. When a child removed one of the poems, he replaced it with another. I read poetry from kid-friendly poets like Shel Silverstein, Jack Prelutsky and Judith Viorst (my favorite) to the students during their library times. Circulation statistics from the poetry section soared. Even the tough audience, boys, became involved.

The Grand Prize was an all-expenses-paid visit to the school by poet-anthologist Lee Bennett Hopkins, the magazine's editor of poetry. In addition to speaking with students, Lee invited me, my principal, and three of my colleagues to dinner with him. I chose the elegant restaurant Caruso's where Bob and I had met. The atmosphere was perfect.

That same mannequin was a permanent fixture in the LRC, changing costumes during different seasons and portraying various book characters. A display of appropriate books was gathered around her for check-out by students and teachers. I had searched the integrated card catalog under "subject" for books on Halloween, Thanksgiving, Christmas, mystery, Easter, e.g., purchased and attached colorful spine label symbols (black cat for Halloween, etc.) which made it easy for kids and teachers, too, to choose a book, without doing a lot of research. Non-fiction books from the 394 Dewey-numbered holiday section were included along with fiction story books. My libraries were always well-marked for ease of use by patrons.

In those early ten years in Houston, I won 12 of 14 competitive grants. The chances of winning were about 30% in most cases. I am blessed with the gift of creativity, write passably, and can motivate students.

Of the awards, I am most proud of being the honoree for a Texas PTA Life Membership. What that award says to me was that I was appreciated by parents for providing their children with enriching, educational experiences. The award is often presented to principals, but I snagged that one, courtesy of the PTA president, who knew what was going on in the library program in one of my last schools before retirement.

In 1998, when the road to divorce was apparent, I moved from the home Bob and I had been sharing. Our house sold in a short period of time, so there was subsistence money to lease a townhouse. I began looking for a job before I moved. It took ten months for a library job to open. I know it was meant to be because the job became available in February of a school year. The librarian in a high school accepted the position of Director of Libraries in the district.

I was in charge of the Media Center in a school of 1,200+ ninth through twelfth graders, my first experience with big kids. I had two library assistants, both of whom were technologically competent. The school primarily served a mobile population near an army base. Because of the mobility, all the textbooks in the school were on the library's database for accountability.

With the primary focus of the previous library staff on technology, the library's book collection had suffered, apparently for years. The shelves were crammed with books, many of them outdated, out of circulation (judging by signatures and dates on the check-out cards), or having multiple copies of a title when one copy would suffice. The collection needed weeding, and books needed repair. There was no instructional signage on the shelves indicating Dewey categories or lettering on the fiction shelves to indicate the first letter of authors' last names and where those books began. One would have to read across several shelves to find the book being sought before the signage.

I literally rolled up my sleeves and moved shelves of books to make way for new additions after weeding the collection. When weeding books from the shelves, they were not thrown into the trash but boxed and sent to the warehouse to be sold when the district had its annual sale to the public of discarded furniture and equipment.

I remained in the position for the remainder of that school year and the next year. I had tremendous support from Jaime, the assistant principal and chairman of the library personnel selection committee. He had the final decision for me to remain the following school year.

Because I was being paid as a "new" teacher with one year's experience due to the time gap since prior employment, I was having difficulty making a living. I had a Master's degree and 16 years of experience at the time. I chose to move back to Houston in 2000, given credit for my degree and years of experience, at a considerable raise in pay.

Over the telephone, I inquired of a former Houston parent volunteer, who was hired as the librarian in the school I had left in 1992, if she knew of any openings in the district. She said that a new charter school, ultimately to be grades 6-12, was opening that fall. The school was under the aegis of my former district and was to focus on technology, business, foreign language, and different cultures.

I was interviewed by several persons over the telephone and got the job. I was a perfect fit with my knowledge of cultures from traveling, the experience I had in setting up a new library facility, and certification in the state of Texas. The school was state-of-the-art with all new technology and a beautiful Media Center. This academy now has an International Baccalaureate program and has won various awards for excellence. According to the school's website, there are almost 1,000 students.

After three years there, I retired from public education. It was time for me to do so. For a year, I worked on starting my own business of giving (as it turned out) multi-media presentations on different cultures to middle/high school students. I marketed to PTA organizations in the district, for they would be the ones paying my fee. I also gave freebies to different community organizations. After that period of time, I realized that the "business" was not going to be viable.

And how did I come to choose a career in library science after not much of a background during my years of growing up? In retrospect, I attribute my wise choice to examination of my natal chart done by an astrologer here in Charlotte. As I re-listened to the CD recording of the reading done August 10, 2010 by Jim, a talented, intuitive astrologer, certain phrases jumped out at me as I took written notes.

Although my sun sign is Cancer (sensitive, imaginative, intuitive, caring, practical, home-loving), my ascendant is Leo, a fire sign. I am self-assured, generous, spontaneous, optimistic, and a lover of the arts, literature and music.

Jim said that personalities are more like their ascendant sign. I have 4 planets in Leo (the sign that appears most frequently) at the time of my birth, with only 2 in Cancer. Leo is considered "the movie star." I loved to dress in costume and be the center of attention; a ham actor. I am a joiner and need to be with people. I am not a shy Cancerian. Although I am an extrovert, I also need reflective time alone to rejuvenate. I have a creative nature.

With two houses in Gemini, an air sign, I have a facility for reading, writing, and speaking. Things mental are a turn-on. I am a risk-taker, love learning, and am a high-energy person.

The Moon is the ruler of the sun sign of Cancer. My moon is in Pisces, giving me a sweet, intuitive nature. Because I am sensitive, I am tuned into people, little ones in particular. I can sense mischief before it develops.

So what does the above mean? I believe that our natal chart gives an indication of our strengths and weaknesses and the careers for which we are best-suited. The more we know about ourselves, the wiser the choices we can make. I chose well.

If you are interested, the following are resources you may want to check. If you want to have a natal chart done and do not know an astrologer, a chart can be ordered at www.arecatalog.com. The A.R.E. is the Association for Research and Enlightenment, founded by medical intuitive Edgar Cayce. I had a chart done there. Jim interpreted this chart and did not need to construct another from square one. The A.R.E. chart is colorful and easy to read. The only information you need for a chart to be done is date of birth, time, and place. This info is on your birth certificate.

Annie Lionnet's *The Astrology Directory* (Ivy Press, Limited: 2003) is a spiral-bound, concise, tabbed reference to esoteric astrology jargon.

A detailed book on astrology is one by Jan Spillar and Karen McCoy, *Spiritual Astrology: A Path to Divine Awakening* (Simon and Schuster: 2010). This book goes into depth for those on a spiritual quest in their lives. On her website, www.janspillar.com, a free natal birth chart and mini interpretation can be obtained on-line with your basic information. You do not have to sign-up for other services to receive the chart and interpretation immediately.

For a flavor of eastern astrology, I like Debbie Burns's *Chinese Horoscopes: An Easy Guide to the Chinese System of Astrology* (Lansdowne: 1998). The book tells how 12 animals influence events and personalities born during each animal's year. I am a water sheep, born in 1943, and am compatible on a scale of 5 (1-5) with rabbit. Bob was born in the year of the rabbit, and we were compatible.

Susan Miller's website www.astrologyzone.com is free to access and provides a detailed, monthly forecast for each sign. Susan is one of Jim's favorite astrologers, and I have found accuracy several times related to what is happening in my life.

I find astrology fascinating, although I still have much to learn about it and its esoteric language.

7.
Travel

*F*ollowing is a partial list of travel adventures, most of them with Bob; some of the trips are pre-or-post Bob:

Thailand (1967)

Canada (British Columbia, Alberta, Manitoba, Ontario and Quebec provinces) various dates

Caribbean (1985)

British Isles and western Europe (late 1980's)

Scandinavia (1990)

Russia (1993)

Israel and Egypt (1994)

Alaska (1995)

Australia and New Zealand (1996)

Greece and Turkey (1997)

Ireland (2000, 2002, 2007)

Peru (2003)

Kenya (2005)

Mexico (2011)

Costa Rica (2013)

I have also traveled and/or lived in every state of the U.S. with the exception of Oregon, Connecticut, and Rhode Island. I list the above places not to impress, but to say that I have had marvelous opportunities to grow in Philos, sometimes bordering Agape, love of so many persons in many lands—to learn we are truly One. We are each Love incarnate. Perhaps some are not aware and have not discovered who they truly are. Discovering who they are does not mean they have to belong to an organized religion. There are deeply spiritual persons in countries that some may consider "backward" or third world. Being a successful, loving person does not mean the ones who have the most material "stuff," live in a fine home, or have an academic degree. These superficial accoutrements mean little in the final analysis, who a person really is.

Because this memoir focuses on Love, I will address those trips during which significant times of love happened.

It was in 1993, just after President Gorbachev's policy of glasnost (openness) became operational, that our large Methodist church in Colorado made contact with a representative of the Russian Peace Foundation to arrange for a group of thirteen of our members to visit Novgorod, Russia. The ancient city was founded in 859 A.D. and is near St. Petersburg. Our visit was the beginning of a dialogue between our two cultures. I don't know if the connection still exists, but we did bring a group of the Russians we visited to Colorado Springs a couple of years later. Our photographer and our Russian guide fell in love, and eventually married.

One of our church members was the CEO of a large hospital system and arranged outdated, but still useful, equipment to be transported to a hospital in Novgorod. Members of our team, including our senior minister, stayed with different families as their space permitted. Our church subsidized the families to pay for expenses incurred like food, transportation, etc. We were allowed two suitcases, one for personal items, the other for medical supplies and gifts.

My family spoke more English than I spoke Russian. Svetlana had a Russian/English dictionary that enabled us to communicate. Body language also spoke for us.

We visited an orphanage while there, other organizations, and places of interest. Russians have a 96% literacy rate and are into the arts of singing, dancing, and literature. The performances the children presented were of professional quality.

My family consisted of Sveta, husband Vova, six-year-old Anton, and Sveta's mother, Olga. When I visited, Olga and Anton (in whose room I stayed) slept in the parents' room. The couple slept on the couch in the living room. The apartment was tiny, a fourth floor walk-up, no elevator.

We had times of camaraderie and laughter like during the banya (bath) on Saturday. No one told me I was to be nude among women and children strangers. If you have not experienced a beating with a birch branch by a hefty Russian woman and been scrubbed raw to increase circulation, and then, after taking a steam sauna, gotten frozen in the snow or an outdoor anteroom, you have not truly lived.

Another memory that shows abundant Philos love was when we visited the parents of Igor, husband of Sveta's cousin Vika. The Russians are family-oriented and evidence the love among members.

I cried as I just re-read the seventeen pages, single-spaced journal I typed up after the trip. I describe Toyla. I quote the following paragraph from page 5:

> I immediately liked Toyla. He is a weathered man, tanned, with twinkling brown eyes full of life. He downs his vodka, after kissing the bottom of the glass to indicate the glass will be empty in one gulp. He was pleased that I imitated his action. I don't know whether it was the vodka or his love of singing that prompted him (and others) to sing several songs, but

I thoroughly enjoyed listening. I sang "Three Blind
Mice for them, after a request that I sing.

Imagine the shock and heartbreak I had for the family when I received a letter from Sveta, about a year later, that said their love child, Anton, had died of a heart condition—lively, dancing Anton. We had played simple games like taking turns putting a finger inside a small, sliding match box, laughing and saying "Ouch!" I loved him.

The Russians were easy to love. Their love was palpable and returned in full by the Americans.

In Australia and New Zealand in 1996, I had begun to think about leaving my marriage to Bob. The age difference was beginning to take its toll, and I used journal writing to sort through my feelings and move toward a decision which would take me two years to make. I saw myself withdrawing from the group of persons, chiefly from our church, which we were leading on the trip Down Under. I began developing a spreading rash on my face. I could not discuss what was happening with me with anyone in the group. While visiting a sheep ranch, I closeted myself in our sleeping quarters for a time. In my angst, I saw a blurring golden light spinning around the top of the room. They were cherubim (the little angels), come to comfort me.

It was in Greece in 1997 that I was becoming closer to making my decision to leave. I wrote about happenings there in Chapter 5 which brought me to the decision I made in 1998.

Ireland is my favorite country on the planet. I have been there three times and would live there if I could. The first visit in 2000 was a short one, part of a tour of the United Kingdom. I traveled with a group but did not have a roommate and had to pay that abominable single supplement charged by tour companies.

The second trip in 2002, before I retired from public education in 2003, was made possible by my winning a $4,600 competitive educational grant to study the country and its culture for two weeks. I came back to the states; created an extensive website for students to consult; gave PowerPoint presentations to several groups; brought back several books by Irish writers and a couple of videos for the school library; and donated the digital camera, which I had purchased for the trip, to the school. I wore my shamrock earrings and Irish linen blouse when I gave the presentations, but could not manage a lilting brogue.

Before I left on the third trip in 2007, after moving to Charlotte, I began having a vision, about a week before I left, of a much-in-love, older peasant couple dancing in a pub in Ireland, singing and laughing. Perhaps they were farmers because of their earlier century dress.

The woman was short, round, and missing a few teeth. She had a scarf on her head, like that of a Russian babushka. The man was tall, slender, and balding. He looked like the actor James Cromwell in the movie about a pig, "Babe." He was wearing a vest, suspenders and knickers. Her skirt was long, and they both had buckles on their worn shoes. They were having a wonderful time together.

It was shortly afterward that I knew that the man was Patrick, who, in this life, was born in Dublin. The woman was me. I believe that I have lived several lives in Ireland. There is a feeling of home each time I visit. My psychic friend Sally, mentioned in Chapter 5, who can read the Akashic Records, confirmed lives of my carefree living there.

I love the Irish people. They are full of life, fun, and sometimes Guinness. They are literary, having produced four Nobel Prize winners in Literature, with a small population of only about 4.5 million persons. The Irish top the number of winners in other countries.

In the times I have been there, there was only one negative experience. It was when I was in a marketplace looking at a stack of apples from which to choose. All of a sudden, there was a rabid woman, screaming (swearing?) at me in what I took to be Gaelic. Perhaps she was fearful that I would be stupid enough to choose one from the bottom of the stack.

The scenery of the country is spectacular. It is said that there are seventeen shades of green in the landscape and rolling hills. The men are large (I like big, smart, hairy guys) and compliment ladies with their charm. Although I do not have Irish blood in this lifetime, my soul is Irish.

We now come to the trip to Peru, the trip I almost did not take. I have always been attracted to sacred sites and wanted to visit Machu Picchu. It was to be my reward upon retirement from public education. Mother had passed in 2002, so there were funds for the trip. I did not realize that it would cost me double the amount I had anticipated. The original amount was to be $3,500. It became $7,000 total. I had paid a large company, which had been in business for a long time and had twenty-two subsidiaries, by check. I learned never to do that again, to pay by credit card where there is recourse in situations like this one.

About a week before I was to leave, I got a letter in the mail saying the company was bankrupt. I was not going anywhere. Eventually, I received compensation from U.S.T.O.A. (U.S. Tour Operators Association) of $190. My travel insurance, which I always purchase, did not cover bankruptcy.

I felt my choices were two—stay home (and cry) or find myself another way to make the trip. I got busy on the Internet and found a company in New York which specializes in South America. I was on a plane the day I was originally scheduled to leave and with a personalized itinerary. It was arranged that I would join some groups, but have my own guide at other times. Having my own guide was a bonus. I got to see the country as a native, not as a tourist. Unfortunately, I did not keep a journal on this trip, and do not remember his name.

One of the highlights of the trip was visiting with a family of my guide's friends—a man, his wife, and their seven-year-old daughter. They did not speak English, and I did not speak Quechua, an indigenous language of the Incas. My guide, their friend, interpreted.

I was invited into their home, a cave-like structure made of earth. There was a platform for sleeping, and 2 or 3 pegs with sparse clothing hanging on them. Outside, there was a large stone that served as their table. My guide handed me a chalk stone. I asked him if it would be o.k. to print my name on their table. He said it would be. I then asked the child to print her name. She looked at me quizzically. The guide said that she did not go to school. Understandable, since they lived in the middle of nowhere. I always felt welcomed by the Peruvian people with whom I came into contact.

The trip to the Machu Picchu site was all I hoped for, even more. Our group took the train from Cusco, once capital of the Incan Empire prior to the early 1500's, to Aguas Calientes, a beautiful resort area at the foot of Machu Picchu. Cusco has an elevation of 11,000 feet, and altitude sickness is common. The symptoms are severe headache, vomiting, nausea and fatigue. Drink the coca tea provided in hotels, hydrate, rest, and, if you can, stay a few days to acclimate to the high elevation before resuming your trip.

Machu Picchu is at an elevation of 8,000 feet. On the 30 minute, winding bus trip to the site, my breath was literally taken away by the beauty of the land. An annoyance at the site is the horde of tourists that make it impossible to think of the grandeur of the place much less to take a photo without another body, coming or going, in the picture. I understand that now the number allowed in on any one day has been limited to preserve the integrity of the site.

Machu Picchu was not vandalized by the Spanish conquistadores, as was much of South America, in the 1530's. It remained hidden within the jungle and was discovered, quite by accident, by American Hiram Bingham in 1911.

I immersed myself in Incan history and culture and gave several presentations to groups after I retired. I began my goal of starting my own business of doing multi-media presentations of cultures to students and community groups, gave a few freebies, and marketed it to PTA organizations within districts which, I had hoped, would pay the fee for my service.

After a gigantic computer crash and no back-up of information, I gave up the dream after about a year. While at my last school, I had asked the tech person to transfer the info on the Ireland website (about twenty pages, and with photos) onto a CD. He saved only the shortcuts, which I did not learn until I retired. All the info and hard work I had completed was on the district's server. It was deleted when I was no longer an employee. With the loss, two of my chief sources of presentation were gone, as was my hope of creating a successful business.

I did continue to travel and produced other PowerPoints to share with groups, as a free service.

In 2005, a team of nine, from our 6,000 member Methodist church in Houston, took a mission trip to Kenya to build a house for a widow and her two children. Muthoni's husband had died of AIDS. She and her children were living in a hut made of dung. We also did painting in the dormitory on a bio-intensive farm in Meru and in the Methodist Hospital and premises in Maua, Kenya. I chose to be a painting detailer since my skills with a hammer were not impressive.

I also had a goal of visiting school libraries and a nursing school library in the area. I had looked into having discarded books from libraries sent by the International Book Project if I could find a sponsor willing to pay shipping expenses. I had contacted Oprah's Angel Network for support since I know Oprah founded and supports a girls' school in South Africa, among other philanthropies. I got a thank-you e-mail in return. Funds were available for non-profits, not individuals.

I was introduced by John, the founder of the bio-intensive farm (which our church supports), to school administrators. John is a community activist who teaches young mothers to grow sustainable foods on small plots of land. The girls stay in the dorm that we upgraded and take classes from John and his compassionate, good-cook wife, Janet.

The many persons we met in Kenya were grateful for the assistance we were providing. I remember a particular time when Doris, our liaison on the hospital staff, and I were walking together outdoors. I began crying, and she was comforting me. I told her that more Americans needed to travel to other countries to see how rich in spirit others are in spite of having few material goods. I have been on trips where some Americans complained about how the country was not like "at home." Perhaps they could not locate a McDonalds and did not like the food in the land in which they were visitors.

What is truly important in life? For me, it is making connections with humanity, showing love, and receiving it in return.

Our group did the "safari" thing on the Maasai Mara the last four days of the trip. According to the 35 page journal we kept, on a round robin basis, and which I offered to transcribe and edit, I tell about what turned out to be a joke on me by the wife of the leader of our group. Bernice said we would be sleeping in tents. I quote from p. 27 of the journal:

> The word "tent" brings visions of sleeping on the ground with crawly or flying insects sharing living quarters with you. The roaring campfire keeps away hungry, assorted beasts. Grub is beans and stout coffee in a porcelain pot prepared over the campfire. The necessary room is behind a scrub bush – Nature's own.

Facilities at the Mara Sarova Lodge were lovely. I had a massage in the spa after all the traveling. The buffets were scrumptious. The hotel showed tourists a quality experience. We saw majestic wildlife up close from the van with an open top for taking photos. I was awed by a lioness and her two cubs that sauntered in front of the van, oblivious to those encroaching on her space. She and her cubs were truly living in the moment, in the "now," an example for us all.

Remember the hullabaloo about the world coming to an end on December 21, 2012? We all know it did not, although it was the end of an age according to the Mayan calendar.

One of best books I've read that describes what was happening is Gregg Braden's *Fractal Time* (Hay House, Inc.: 2009). Gregg is a computer programmer/scientist who merges science with spirituality in an understandable manner. Fractals are patterns in nature that re-occur over eons of time. The process is complicated, but the idea can be grasped with his explanation. I recommend his book if you are interested in this topic. Our universe completed its fifth world age in 2012 and has moved into its sixth.

I heard Gregg speak in Flat Rock, NC a couple of years ago. He spoke for three hours, being energetic, knowledgeable, brilliant, wise, magnetic, and good looking. On his website www.greggbraden.com, he also talks about heart intelligence in the video posted. He has written several other books, and I am a fan of his work.

Near the end of 2011, I was reading Barbara Hand Clow's *The Mayan Code* (Bear and Company: 2007) and her *The Pleiadian Agenda* (Bear and Company: 1995). According to the back cover of *The Mayan Code*, Barbara is a "…Mayan Elder, Cherokee Record Keeper, and internationally acclaimed ceremonial teacher and author. She has written ten other books."

Although I could not locate the exact sentence in the above books that jumped off a page at me, "now is the time for you (and others) to activate Gaia (Mother Earth) according to the Mayan calendar," I felt I was being called to Mayan temple sites, particularly Palenque, in Mexico. At the time, I was not certain what I was to do there. I began researching and studying the Mayan culture and was intrigued by what I was learning.

I found myself on an airplane, landing in Mexico City on December 23, 2011. I traveled with a group across the northern section of the entire peninsula, stopping at a number of temples, and flying out of Cancun on January 1, 2012. When I got back to the states, I created a PowerPoint on the Mayan culture and its territories, and made presentations to various groups, hopefully allaying fears of the perceived "disaster" coming at the end of the year.

My experience at Palenque was remarkable. It was a time of healing for me, and in turn, I believe, for Mother Earth.

Palenque consists of a complex of buildings, with a star attraction being The Temple of the Inscriptions. According to Drunvalo Melchizedek's *Serpent of Light* (Weiser Books: 2008), Palenque, "… besides being the capital of the pineal chakra, (it) is where the active arteries and ley lines of the Feathered Serpent cross."

The most famous Mexican god is Quetzalcoatl (called Kukulcan by the Maya) the plumed serpent, part quetzal bird and part rattlesnake. There are stone depictions of Quetzalcoatl at several sites in Mexico.

Melchizedek continues:

"Palenque sits at the edge of the Peten Jungle in the state of Chiapas, a huge area southwest of the Yucatan. It is many things: the Pleiadian Hall of Records, a mystery school of sacred geometry, (and) a major archaeoastronomical center."

Recently, while I was reading Christine Day's *Pleiadian Principles for Living* (Career Press, Inc.: 2013), the following sentences made an impact, and I knew that I had accomplished what I felt called to do in Palenque:

On 11/11/11, there was a dynamic shift (of energy). Waves of a birthing light anchored onto the planet. The energies that came at that time brought a frequency of love that created new avenues for each one of you to move through.

This is the ritual I performed. I sat in the lotus position, on the ground, in front of the Temple of Inscriptions which had been the tomb of the great Mayan king Pakal, who lived in the seventh century and ruled for 68 years. His tomb was discovered in 1952.

I closed my eyes and began to breathe rhythmically, in through my nose and out from my mouth. As I felt myself surrender to the meditation, I envisioned a white light of energy spiraling down from Source, through me, and into Mother Earth. Then the light circled up from Mother Earth, through me, and back to Source. The final visualization was seeing the light coming from both directions, meeting in the middle of my heart chakra, then spiraling outward in all directions.

I raised my arms, and with hand movements, softly sang, "I am that I am, has sent me, in this now moment, here I am. I am that I am, has sent me, in this now moment, here I am. To be the voice, and to be the heart, through which heaven is made known on earth." It is a song which we had sung in my church, Unity. I then began telepathically apologizing to Mother Earth for all the indignities humanity has inflicted upon her—overpopulation, violence, wasting natural resources, pollution—whatever came to my mind. The time was an emotional, heartfelt experience. It was a time of love and healing for Mother Earth and me, with my having gone through the pancreatic cancer and subsequent chemo experiences that very year.

When I returned to the bus, I looked in the mirror of my cosmetic compact, and saw two eyes, wet with tears and smeared mascara. The two black eyes were a fitting symbol of our treatment of our Mother, whom I believe is a sentient being.

I also find it interesting to note that Melchizedek calls Palenque the "capital of the pineal chakra." The pineal chakra is what mystics call "the third eye" which is located in the center of the forehead. That chakra is the energy center of insight, wisdom, imagination, and intuition, according to one Internet source.

If you are interested in doing chakra clearing and meditation, Shirley MacLaine's VHS *Inner Workout* (High Ridge Productions: 1988), although it is 26 years old, is available on www.half.com. This website is a subsidiary of eBay, but requires no bidding. It is a favorite resource of mine when I am looking for various resources.

The final trip I wish to address in this chapter that has to do with love and compassion for others is the trip to Costa Rica a few months ago. Again, I did not know why I chose to take the trip other than I had heard the country has gorgeous scenery. Costa Rica is hot and humid, like Charlotte and Houston, and was not high on my list of places to visit.

On the trip, I met a gentleman who had lost his wife of many years, just seven months prior. He was in deep grief and was hurting. As we came to know one another, he indicated that he was interested in a relationship. He was bright and an interesting conversationalist. I appreciated a companion during the trip, but that was all.

With my training and experience as a hospice volunteer, I listened as he shared. When I got back to the states, I sent him Dr. Weil's *Sound Body, Sound Mind* CD and a few books I thought might be helpful to him. Receipt ($40 spent) of the materials was not acknowledged, and I never heard from him again. I hope, in some small way, that the compassion I offered helps him to heal on his journey.

FATHER'S UNIDENTIFIED FAMILY MEMBERS

DOLORES'S MATERNAL FAMILY

MOTHER'S 70TH BIRTHDAY

PAT AND DOLORES'S WEDDING

PRINCESSES RHONDA AND DONNA
/ DONNA AND RHONDA

TWEEDLE DUM AND TWEEDLE DEE

EGYPTIAN MAN AND CLEOPATRA

BOB, STUDIOUS PROFESSOR

HOUSE IN CREEDE, COLORADO

SAL AND ME ON A JANUARY PICNIC IN COLORADO

MY PEN PAL, LOIS, 93

MY RUSSIAN FAMILY

TREE HUGGING IN NEW ZEALAND

MEDITATING ON THALASSO SEA IN GREECE

MAUA GIRLS' SCHOOL, KENYA

MUTHONI'S NEW HOUSE IN KENYA

MAASAI WARRIOR WITH LION'S MANE HAT, KENYA

TEMPLE OF INSCRIPTIONS, PALENQUE, MEXICO

8.
Health and Other Challenges

As I thought about what I wanted to include in this chapter, I felt a sense of heaviness and depression. I do not feel that I have been a victim over the past four years. I know that everything happens for a reason in life. When I awoke at 5:30 A.M. yesterday (my usual waking time), I received an inspiration. I know it was from my angels. Why not include some starlight after each "problem" as I coped, solved, accepted, lived through, or healed? Thus, you will see action following three stars (* * *) for assistance on my journey.

I summarized tests and procedures here and left out dates noted on my "Med Procedures" Word documents saved since 2007. I have synthesized years 2010-2013. Also know that I have omitted reference to routine doctors' visits to my primary care, dentist, ophthalmologist, gynecologist, orthopedic surgeon, oncologist, chiropractor and other medical professionals which do not relate to the subject being discussed. I adore (respect) five of the seven physicians listed above. Why is it that some men seemingly "have it all" — looks, personality, education, compassion, money, wives?

Medical/Health Challenges

Diabetes and Hip Injury

In 2000, I was diagnosed with non-insulin dependent diabetes. My glucose and blood pressure are high, chiefly, I believe, because I am in chronic pain over the past year and one-half due to trochanteric bursitis and have difficulty walking and exercising. With the serious falls I have endured, the bursa sac on my left hip is inflamed from the injuries. The left side of my neck and left shoulder project pain in addition to the hip problem. I have headaches daily.

* * *

In July of this year, my primary care doctor did not see evidence of an advanced arthritic condition, nor bone on bone, on an x-ray. Over the past year, I have had seven appointments with a chiropractor whose means of treatment was the roller bed, stimulator, and acupressure. I received some relief from acupuncture. It was not covered by insurance. The fee of $49 per treatment was not in my budget. Next stop was asking my primary care doctor for a referral to an orthopedic surgeon. This doctor gave me cortisone shot and said if the injury did not heal in six weeks to report to the Hip and Knee Center uptown. He indicated no interest in treating me further.

The end of September, I was in Staples for an advertised free computer tune-up. Chiropractors were in the front of the store doing a promo for their office—x-rays and consultation for a nominal fee. I have gone to chiropractors for over 20 years, with varying results.

I liked the two doctors, and since healing was at a stand-still for me, I signed up for an appointment.

I am committed to a five-month plan of treatment. My insurance picks up some of the cost, but there is a substantial sum that I am to pay out of my pocket, so much per month for 18 months. I like the philosophy of the here unnamed company. Only about 1% of chiropractors focus on the five essentials of mind over body (power to self-heal); toxin reduction; oxygenation through exercise; nutrition; and blood supply to nerves. I asked the doctor who owns the practice how I could oxygenate in addition to taking deep breaths (with my difficulty walking). His reply to my question about smoking a hookah water pipe (since water is hydrogen and oxygen) was that he wanted to join my party. We both laughed. I am hoping the hip heals from the nerve damage. In any case, I know from x-rays that my neck is losing its curve and my hips are uneven. If the condition is not addressed with adjustments, the spinal disks will fuse, and I will lose range of motion over time. I am not in fear but know the condition needs attention. I was given an all-natural analgesic cream for pain which I apply twice a day. It helps.

Most medications have toxic side effects. I no longer take, with my primary doctor's knowledge, the blood pressure med which caused severe itching all over my body for two years. Also out is the anti-depressant which turned me into a zombie for a year. The statin for lowering cholesterol caused me to lose my memory as I noticed when playing the game of bridge. The sleeping med is evil, as I observed personally and heard stories from many others. Although it is still on the market (pharmaceutical lobbying?), the recommended dosage has been cut in half, I learned from a speaker with a Ph.D. in pharmacy when I asked the question why was it still on the market. The potent, prescribed pain meds make me loopy. I will cope with the pain with, as Dr. Brian, my chiropractor recommended, a rotation of aspirin, acetaminophen, and ibuprofen. Long-term use of aspirin affects the stomach; acetaminophen, the kidneys; and ibuprofen, the liver.

I know a fair amount about nutrition and received additional tips from Dr. Brian. Recently, since I do not have access to a cow and unadulterated milk, I am switching to almond and coconut milks. Ezekiel flourless bread, composed of sprouts of four grains, is replacing white bread. I tried a couple of natural sweeteners which do not work for my taste buds. I told my chiropractor and my primary care doctors that since I have not eaten red meat products for seventeen years; do not smoke, drink alcohol or do recreational drugs; and do not have sex that French fries are a culinary necessity.

For those wondering about weight loss or the glycemic index of carbohydrate rapid-inducers of insulin, for diabetics particularly, in Appendix H of Dr. Barry Sears's *Enter the Zone* (HarperCollins: 1995), four pages of foods are listed with percentages. A low percentage is best.

I am concentrating on healing my body. I find Louise Hay's emphasis on positive affirmations helpful in her book *You Can Heal Your Life* (Hay House: 1999). Hay House is her successful publishing company which counts numerous well-known authors on metaphysical topics. I excerpt maladies, ones with which I am dealing, and the positive, healing affirmation. There are 45 pages of information on the topic of problems experienced.

Problem: Diabetes

Probable cause: Longing for what might have been. A great need to control. Deep sorrow. No sweetness left.

New Thought Pattern: This moment is filled with joy. I now choose to experience the sweetness of today.

Problem: Hip Problems

Probable cause: Fear of going forward in major decisions. Nothing to move forward to.

New Thought Pattern: I am in perfect balance. I move forward in life with ease and with joy at every age.

Problem: Pancreas

Probable cause: Represents the sweetness of life.

New Thought Pattern: My life is sweet.

Another healing technique I use is Ho'oponopono, according to an article by Sean M. Adams on the Internet, it

"...is an ancient Hawaiian practice of reconciliation and forgiveness which, when we take the time to acknowledge that we are in pain and that we need to move forward and heal we can open ourselves to more abundance and prosperity. When you release the pain of the hurt and open your heart and self to forgiveness you prepare yourself to be able to receive all the goodness that is coming your way...."

When I first learned of the technique was several years ago in a book by Joe Vitale of *The Secret* movie fame. Adams's definition sounds like it clears emotional pain. I am using it to clear physical pain by saying the four-fold message Vitale gave, while touching my left hip: "I'm sorry. Please forgive me. Thank you. I love you."

I also frequently implore Archangel Raphael, who is a healer of human and animal bodies, to speed my recovery.

Other medical challenges

Following is a synthesis of tests, procedures, and doctor visits from 2010-2013. The number following each entry is for the number of times it occurred. The list is not all inclusive. It does represent substantial financial outlay for me, despite insurance coverage. I choose to have medical expense itemized on taxes and maintain an Excel spreadsheet each year.

- Elevated liver enzymes and severe body itching (3)

- Emergency room visits (3)

- Stitches in palm due to a fall in the bathtub

- Fractured right humerus due to a fall in a parking lot with uneven asphalt

- Chills and abdominal pain for 16 hours

- Physical therapy and right arm in sling for 10 weeks. No driving

- Falls (5)

- Other falls happened on stairs in my home other than two major ones in tiled bathrooms, 6 days apart during the night, in Costa Rica in March. These were due to a prescribed sleeping medication. I did not realize that I had fallen the second night until I saw blood in my hair and on the pillow that A.M. My coccyx took 6 weeks to heal.

- Ultrasounds (2)

- Endoscopies (2) to remove gallstones and a stent

- X-rays (5)

- CT-scans (6)

- EKG (2)

- Pancreatic surgery in April, 2011. 11 days in hospital

- Power Port for chemo meds installed. Has to be flushed by the nurse every 6 weeks

- Chemo treatments for 6 months

- Naturopathic treatment by N.D. for 6 weeks

- Chiropractic treatments sporadically since 2007

I think it appropriate to include here an unpublished article on the pancreatic cancer experience which I wrote in July, 2011.

Pancreatic Cancer Surgery:
Positive Mind-Set vs. Reality

After ten months of appointments with physicians, multiple tests and bills, I was diagnosed with pancreatic cancer on March 18, 2011. On April 11, I underwent, according to my 63-page medical record (April 11-22), a "Whipple Procedure with Intra Operative Ultrasound Diagnostic Laparoscopy." The complex procedure was invented by American surgeon Allen Whipple in 1935 and is widely used by skilled surgeons in treating pancreatic cancer. During the Whipple, the tumor on the head of my pancreas, gall bladder, duodenum, and a biliary duct were removed, along with a re-sectioning of my small intestine. It is a major surgery.

With my positive mind-set, I do not give in to the depressing, negative statistics given by the American Cancer Society's Cancer

Facts & Figures 2010 report. Pancreatic cancer has the highest mortality rate of all major cancers with 94% of those diagnosed predicted to die within five years and 75% dying within the first year. Surgical removal of the tumor is possible in only about 15% of those diagnosed because there are no detection tools in its early stages. It is an aggressive disease and woefully underfunded, receiving only 2% of the National Cancer Institute's approximate $5 billion cancer research budget for the year. I choose to be in the minority 6% with my positive outlook for my future. I am a survivor.

Two helpful websites dealing with this cancer are www.pancan.org, which offers a free packet of materials to help manage diagnosis and learn about pancreatic cancer. Another is www.lustgarten.org, which has a long list of Information and Support Services. Caring Bridge is a free, interactive website to enable updates and well wishes for those facing health issues. The Lustgarten Foundation is a major fund raiser for the cause of pancreatic cancer and welcomes donations on its website.

Reality

Underestimating the severity of the procedure and the recovery time. I have heard it said that for each day spent in the hospital, there is a one-week recovery period. Mine will be about twelve weeks, i. e., about three months.

Suffering the side effects of drugs given. Side effects I experienced are the following:

- **Dizziness:** Dilaudid, Reglan, OxyContin

- **Constipation:** Dilaudid, OxyContin, Morphine

- **Headache:** Reglan, OxyContin, Morphine

- **Dry mouth:** Dilaudid, Celexa, OxyContin

- **Itching:** Dilaudid, OxyContin, Morphine

- **Hallucinations:** Dilaudid, Celexa, Reglan, Morphine

- **Nausea/vomiting:** Celexa, Reglan, OxyContin, Morphine

- **Blurred vision:** Morphine

I was told that the near death experience (N.D.E.) I had was caused by the hallucinogens – maybe, but probably not. On the second day after the surgery, three MDs, one PA, and one RN/BSN were standing in my room. In the upper left corner of the room, I said I saw "something." I did not say angel, but I knew it was because I am clairsentient. That night, I saw myself walking toward the Light. There was such peace and love; but I knew I had a decision to make. I said, "I am not finished here yet." I "awoke" screaming, "I want to go back! I want to go back!" There was pain like I've never known. The screaming brought several persons to my bedside asking my pain level. I said 8, but it was more like 11.5 on a scale of 1-10. There was a nurse standing to my left, hands on her hips, telling me to quiet down. I was disturbing other patients. I looked her steadily in the eyes, called her by name, and said, "You are so cold."

Being awakened at 12:30 A.M., 2:30 – 3:00 A.M, and 5:30 A.M. for medications, finger sticks, vitals, etc.

Getting a large pill stuck in my throat (with the tube) for several hours when awakened during the night. I was supine, and the attending nurse did not ask me to sit up to take the medication.

Grimacing with pain when the gastric bag fell, yanking the eraser-size incision in my side. The tube was connected to the abdominal area to drain excess fluid. A kind nurse finally pinned the apparatus to my gown to hold it in place. Now to be careful not to lie on it amid all the other tubes attached to me.

Waiting one hour, and, at another time, 40 minutes for a nurse to answer my call light.

Receiving conflicting instruction about self-administered pain medication. One nurse told me to press the pain button every five minutes. The next day, I learned that I had pressed the button 80 times. Meds cut off after a certain amount is requested.

Being uncomfortable with the gastric tube down my throat for six days. It was taken out briefly until I vomited the good-tasting bites of salmon I had one evening. Good going down, not so good coming up. Fortunately, the tube was removed permanently on the Sunday I had many visitors.

Bruising of my tailbone due to multiple days in bed on my back. All the attached tubes made other positions difficult. I had brought a neck pillow, which I positioned under my hips with the opening providing some relief for the tailbone.

Having an uneven quality of care. Some medical personnel were conscientious, others not.

Being subjected to noise at all hours during the day and into the evening. One night, there was a visiting small child across the hall screaming at 10:00 P.M. I called the supervising nurse to take care of this incident.

Wailing on the toilet and straining to have a bowel movement two days before I was discharged. It had been thirteen days since I had had one. One small drop was managed; the next day, three, with considerable pain. My daughter intimated, jokingly, that since I was not nice to the nurse on duty, she gave me a double dose of laxative to get even! I had to deal with the after effects of the "joke" for two days after arriving home.

Positives:

Asking the anesthesia RN to play Dr. Andrew Weil's healing CD "Sound Body, Sound Mind" through my earphones during the operation. Dr. Weil does a short introductory healing meditation. The remainder of the CD contains beautiful selections of music that enable the listener to go within to the body's healing center to heal itself. It's ok to fall asleep. I had listened to the CD several times before entering the hospital. She arranged for my request to be honored.

Receiving forty-three cards and well wishes from family, friends, church members, and others.

Enjoying nine floral/plant arrangements in the hospital and sent to my home. Before the surgery, I received a lovely arrangement from my ex-husband and his wife. When I telephoned to thank him, I said, "What? We've been divorced twenty-seven years and NOW you send me flowers?!" We both laughed.

Having eleven visitors, bearing gifts, on the first Sunday after the surgery. I was feeling human because the gastric tube had been removed that morning.

Receiving telephone calls so numerous that I had to empty the memory on my answering machine twice. There were twenty that day. The only disadvantage to all the calls is that I have a land line, no cellular phone. The phone is not near the couch. By the time I could upright myself, the caller had hung up or had left a message. I was not feeling well enough for conversation; however, it was gratifying to know others were thinking of me.

Experiencing the healing prayer circle formed by Unity chaplains around me after service the Sunday before the surgery and the powerful prayers they said with their hands upon me.

Knowing that I was being prayed for by dozens of persons who told me so.

Crying with emotion as the Unity music team, dedicated to me, and sang, Ricky Skaggs's "Somebody's Praying" the first Sunday I returned to church. The video of the song's performance by Skaggs can be found on YouTube by researching "Ricky Skaggs's Somebody's Praying."

Being told, by several persons, that I am a role model of courage and love. It is not my purpose to tout the Unity faith (**www.unity.org**), but to say that, for me, the love and support of this group (who believe in the efficacy of prayer; the oneness of humanity and divinity; alternative healing modalities; positive mind-set; and the power of love) pulls me from the abyss of the ordeal I faced, and am facing. Our mission statement, repeated each Sunday is "to inspire and encourage spiritual living in a world awakening to love." Their love and support is like none I have known.

Chemo begins June 8. The journey of life continues.

Sources

"Pancreatic Cancer Facts." American Cancer Society, 2010. Web.

http://www.pancreatic.org

Weil, Andrew, M.D., Perf. "Sound Body, Sound Mind." Warner Music Group: 1997, C.D.

My friend Sally died of pancreatic cancer this past June. She had a Whipple the year before I did and had two re-occurrences.

* * *

There are so many positives in what seemingly was a negative experience, certainly the most difficult time in my 70 years of life. But I coped, lived through it, healed and became an inspiration to others. My courage increased exponentially. If I could get through that challenge, I can face and conquer the vicissitudes which arise. I expect, when I see my oncologist for my 6-month visit in January that I remain cancer-free in year three. I am a survivor, and my work on this planet is not yet finished.

The Saga of the Sod

I live in a townhome community which employs a management company to which I pay the highest of three-level fees because my unit has 2.5 bathrooms. I am not impressed with the company. The ratio paid, to benefit received, is low. But I need not go into all the reasons.

In March of this year, I was tired of the hassle of having scarce grass in the backyard that slopes and allows dirt to flow onto the patio when it rains. I have lived here for seven years. Neither was the grass in the front yard a showplace. I take pride in my property inside and outside. There would be no assistance from the management company or their landscaper.

In spite of being on a fixed income, I came up with $800 to have sod installed on the back and front yards. The yard looked great for three weeks. At the advice of the man who did the work, I called the office of the landscape contractor employed by the association and had their workers refrain from mowing my lawn for that period of time. Then along came the behemoth riding mower with dull cutting blades which pulled out chunks of the grass, and, in essence, killed the fresh sod in front and back. I had asked the supervisor to have the men use a powered walk-behind mower which was less stressful to the new lawn. Then the company began to skip mowing my yard altogether. What was left of the grass had grown several inches. I called the landscaper's office several times. With my research background, I found the owner of the company and wrote to him. He returned the letter, unopened.

* * *

In spite of my frustration, I learned that I am not responsible for that person's cowardice.

A Surprise from the Internal Revenue Service

It was in 2011 that I received a greeting from the I.R.S. which informed me that my taxes for 2009 had been audited and that I owed $17,000. What?! Then the letter from the NC Department of Revenue arrived. They had jumped on the bandwagon and said that I owed them several thousand as well.

In 2010 and a couple of years before, I had gone to the Senior Center to have my taxes done by persons who had taken the Tax Aide class. For a donation, it is a fine service for older persons who either cannot, or have no interest, in filing their own taxes. Since I always had a husband, or someone else, do the taxes, I had no reason to suspect that the person had no experience in filling out a Schedule D form for capital losses on my modest inheritance.

* * *

I went to a professional tax preparer and had an amended federal and state return filed. I will continue to go to a professional preparer in the future in spite of the cost for itemized returns.

Townhouse for Sale

In May of this year, I began shredding files I no longer needed and began downsizing. I am an organized person, not a collector. I just felt this urge to simplify. I had no thought of moving at the time.

On August 10, I decided to put my townhouse on the market since home sales were moving upward. I contacted my very competent, likeable agent, Susan, who had sold me this property seven years ago when I moved from Houston. At the time, I did not know a soul here, but I was ready for an adventure. I visited Charlotte a couple of times – unfortunately, not during the summer months. Within a year of my moving here, each of my two daughters moved to Charlotte, and they remain here.

I have grown tired of living in Charlotte with its conservative religious ideas, sports mania, and political drama. The city received good press during the Democratic National Convention, and people began moving here in droves. Tailgaters, many with out-of-state plates on their cars, abound. North Carolina has the distinction of being on a top ten list of states with the worst drivers. I do not remember the agency which conducted the recent poll.

I usually drive the speed limit in the far right lane, not poking along. I am not fazed by fingers and angry shouts from other motorists. If I sense intense anger, I send a blessing of white light to the driver. The time I tapped on my brake when I had an 18-wheeler truck on a freeway traveling at a high speed on my bumper, and he zoomed past me in the left lane, and slammed on his brakes — that fazed me.

I am ready for a smaller, cooler-climate town near the mountains in western Carolina. I read about Asheville, where I visited and would like to live, but it is expensive there. Hendersonville, twenty-five miles south of Asheville, feels perfect for me.

I found an agent there, looked at property, and signed a contingency contract on a place I liked. Basically, the contract said that when my house sells, I'll buy yours. That contract expired on October 15. The house was free-standing (no shared walls). It had a one-car garage and driveway (no community parking lot) to protect Natalie Nissan (the name of my car) and provide a place for storing Christmas decorations and yard implements. Having a one story house (no stairs to crawl up or on which to fall) attracted me over a house with two stories. It had two bedrooms and two bathrooms, a patio deck, and a separate sun room. A fireplace was a requirement and that one was gas-vented, thus no buying firewood and having a smoky odor in the house after a wood-fueled fire.

Although the place was built in 1985, there had been some upgrades. Painting was not a big project, and my agent Diane knew a painter. Taxes were lower than they are in Charlotte, although the association fee was a bit higher. There was a berm behind the unit providing privacy. The grounds were well-maintained. I thought it was going to be my home. There was a pool with gradual steps down that I could use, unlike the one in this complex which I pay to maintain.

I had contacted movers and had gotten three estimates. I applied for, and received, pre-approval on financing a new loan. I even picked out paint samples for my new house to be. It is now almost the year 2014, and I am still in Charlotte.

* * *

I realize now that the Universe is in charge of my life; our plans did not synchronize at first. Although I was crushed with disappointment when the Hendersonville contract fell through, I believe I am given these additional months to write this manuscript and have it published. I am meant to delay having to pack and move and find new favorite physicians. I will also have the services of my hair-stylist extraordinaire, Karen, and Frankie, my manicurist who does not cause me pain when doing my nails. When the house sells, I believe in the spring, I will have money to move; the small down payment required; closing costs; and the funds to contract the publisher for this manuscript.

I am accepting what is, and what is to be, as linear time moves on.

Betrayal

On www.dictionary.com, the word "betray" has five definitions. I am choosing the meaning: "to disappoint the hopes or expectations of; to be disloyal to" to address this challenge in my life. Betrayal has only happened in a big way four times in my life — with my father, my first husband, and two once-close friends.

You have read the story of my childhood experience with my father, and were probably able to infer the experience with my first husband. I had expected fidelity in my marriage and was devastated that it did not happen.

The third time came when Bob and I separated. We were in a group in Colorado Springs of age 50+ senior couples called the "Hilltoppers" who socialized together. There were four Bobs and wives among group members. Once we all went to a Bob Fest together where one could purchase a T-shirt with the wording "I'm with Bob" with arrows pointing in two directions. The group had light-hearted times together.

Elaine, wife of a Bob, was my second best friend in the city. We had met in 1991 when she, as a realtor, sold us the house in Briargate. Elaine was bubbly, and she and I got along fabulously. Many persons in the group said that Bob and I were the perfect couple. We shared family occasions with Elaine and Bob, including Thanksgiving dinners and their daughter's wedding.

One day in 1998, Elaine dropped by and saw the living room with several packed boxes. It was just before I was separating from Bob. I had not told anyone in the group because I thought they would not understand with Bob and I being "the perfect couple." Maybe there was fear that if Bob and I were breaking up, it could happen in their marriage. That was speculation. I don't know. Elaine's husband was grumpy and put her down in front of others.

I stopped getting invites, and Bob's side was the one taken. I thought Elaine's and my friendship was stronger than it turned out to be. After I had left for Houston in 2000, I telephoned once and left a message. Perhaps the message was not passed on by someone who played the message, or perhaps Elaine chose not to return the call. There was the pain of loss, but, in time, I did heal from it.

I returned to Houston in 2000. It was near impossible to live on the salary I was making in Colorado, that of a beginning teacher with one year's experience, when, in reality, I had sixteen years of experience in schools and a Master's degree.

I tried to renew my friendship with Lois. Lois and Jim were the witnesses when Bob and I married in 1985. Lois and I were BFFs. We saw each other often and shared girl secrets. She and Jim had gotten married about two years before Bob and I did.

When Jim told Lois he wanted a divorce, I was there for her. When she telephoned with the devastating news, I packed a picnic lunch and went over to her house. We sat in the middle of her living room floor, eating little. I listened and comforted her the best way I could.

Our relationship never renewed when I returned to Houston after my divorce. I tried, but it appeared our time together as friends was over.

* * *

For those of you who have experienced betrayal, you know it is a painful experience. Perhaps you know, too, that we move on from those times. We can forgive (forgiveness is for the one making the decision to do so), but we need not forget. Getting rid of anger or resentment heals our own selves.

I did not have the ceremony that I did when forgiving my father, but I did forgive those persons whom I have mentioned. Time together with each was over, and I realized that I needed to move forward to let others into my heart.

Technology

If I could just sit and write with pen and paper, there would be less frustration. Although I am computer literate, I am not an expert. I have had two crashes since beginning this writing project six weeks ago, and I have had to step away for a day or two from writing to mentally recover. For a while, I questioned whether I was meant to complete this undertaking. But then I sat down in front of this machine again. I need not go into all the details I have encountered and endured.

* * *

I had more memory installed on this computer which is only 2-3 years old—obsolete, I know. Scott of Staples did his tech thing and took care of the hardware.

I paid for one hour of tutoring, during their store's busy season, with Sean and Cynthia of the UPS Store. Their experience exceeds my own. Had I not done so, I would have been at a standstill. They will also help with manipulation of the photos to be included. I know a bit of technique in this area since I have created several PowerPoint presentations with photos in the past.

My neighbor Barbara was a computer tech for 20 years in her career. She came over Friday and gave me more tips. I am doing fine, and the yelling at inanimate equipment is decreasing.

Loneliness

In the sixteen years since my separation and divorce from Bob, I have dated little—like a few first dates, period. At different times, I have been a short-term member in a couple of the large, on-line dating services. I have also spent un-quality time on about three smaller sites.

When I moved to Charlotte (and not knowing a soul here), I joined one of the "biggies" for three months. When I noticed the company had charged me for months more on my credit card,

I called to protest. I had not found the secret place on the website that would have turned the automatic renewal off. I asked the young woman who answered the telephone, "Why would I pay for such a pathetic experience?" We laughed, and she removed the charge from my credit card account.

The holidays are a difficult time for me. I have no close girlfriends in this city (besides my two daughters who are busy in their lives) and nowhere to wear my fabulous holiday wardrobe. Of the last two gentlemen who showed interest in me, one is 80 years old, the other 84. No thanks. My energy level is high, and someone my own age is probably too old for me.

* * *

In November, 2007 (the list has a date) when the Law of Attraction was big, I made a list of the qualities I am looking for in a male companion. It remains in my "It" box as suggested by Esther Hicks who channels the entity Abraham. The Universe is well aware of the qualities I seek, and if fated, will send the perfect mate for me. Notice I said "perfect for me." Perfection in any human is a myth. If, or until, then:

> "You" (I) cannot be lonely if you like the
> person you are alone with." I do.

> Dr. Wayne Dyer

Finances

In addition to escalating living expenses on a fixed income, I am saddled with piles of medical expenses, the remains of which are not covered by insurance. My social security is below $200 a month (although I have 44 quarters of paying into the system, I will not go into why that is so). I took payment at the age of 62 and retired, with a pension from public education, with 21 years of service. I earned social security benefits while working in public libraries, with no retirement system benefits in different states. I did not go into public education with hopes of becoming wealthy. I was required to have an all-level teaching certificate as well as being certified as a Library Media Specialist. I did expect to be able to live and pay for expenses in my retirement years.

Technology expense has also become an issue as I write this manuscript. I tried writing with pencil and paper, which does not work for me.

* * *

I have arranged payment plans with four practices—oncology, a family practice, the dentist, and the chiropractor. Sometimes, payment can be arranged through Care Credit, which is a bank-backed service. If the entire amount is paid within a stipulated time period (a year, perhaps eighteen months), there is no interest charge. It is a way to survive while paying medical bills.

There is small flex account from the investment made from my inheritance into which I "dip" to meet expenses which occur. I am practical with money, and although generous in many ways, I want to pass on as much as possible to my own daughters as my mother did for me.

It is time to move on to a more pleasant chapter to write.

9.
Gifts of Intuition and Moxie

My definition of intuition is an inner knowing; a perception of truth; a gut feeling. I believe we each have psychic ability. It is more highly developed in some persons. In this chapter, I will relate scenarios which I have experienced.

In the mid-1970's, I began reading books on metaphysical and paranormal topics. In the mid-to-late 1980's, I had my first déjà vu experience/vision. I was standing on the bridge to Traitor's Gate at the Tower of London, overlooking the Thames River. It was 4:00 in the afternoon.

All of a sudden, in mind's eye, I saw the scene change. I was observing that it was dawn, perhaps a day in the 1500's. The land and river were at a higher level. There was an air of festivity among the crowd. There was to be a public beheading this day. Vendors were selling wares of pretzels, flowers, and like items. There was music. The dress of the people of that time was consistent with drawings I had seen in books. The vision lasted just a short time, but I was able to take in what was happening.

I have had a fascination with English Tudor history for many years. I have visited England five or six times. I have read extensively about that era, and can even name Henry VIII's six wives, in order, and how they died.

One of the best books I've read on the dynasty, a novel of fictionalized history (as opposed to historical fiction), is a 937-page tome by Margaret George, *The Autobiography of Henry VIII: With Notes by His Fool, Will Somers* (St. Martin's Griffin: 1986). Although it is a novel, it is well-researched and reads easily. There is an impressive family tree of several generations in the front pages of the book.

From the dates recorded in this family history, I learned that Henry ruled from 1509-1547, a total of 38 years. After Henry died, 10 year-old Edward VI, the son of Henry and Jane Seymour, became king and ruled for six years, dying at the age of 16. Edward's mother died in childbirth, and sickly Edward died as a teenager.

Mary, called "Bloody Mary," child of Henry and first wife Katherine of Aragon, ruled for 5 years after Edward died. Henry's "illegitimate" daughter Elizabeth I (with wife Anne Boleyn) then ruled from 1558-1603, a total of 45 years, the Golden Years in English history.

Margaret George has written an equally enchanting biography of Mary, Queen of Scots, Elizabeth's cousin. I have not read her books on Cleopatra and other famous personages.

So many visions have come, unexpectedly, over the years. Some have helped me to understand how or why they relate to my life. I'll share scenarios, in no particular order, here.

Scenario 1

A humorous time happened in the Creede Hotel in Colorado. I'll give a brief background of the town. In the early 1890's, Creede was a boomtown of 10,000 seekers of fortune in mining silver and amethyst. Most were a hard-drinking, rowdy group from all over the known country. There were not many decent women in the town, mostly ladies of the night. There is a mountain in the north part of town called Bachelor Mountain. You get the idea.

When Bob and I were building our cabin outside the small, present-day town, we would stay in the 100+ years-old hotel which had four rooms upstairs. We liked a room on the backside off the street, away from noisy repertory theater goers. The food, as well as the accommodation, was excellent. We got to know Cathy and Rich, the owners, who were year-round residents.

On a balmy summer night, moonlight shined through the open window of our room which faced a hewn mountainside. I was asleep, with covers off my nightgown. It was a warm night, and there was no air-conditioning. I awoke with a slap, slap-slap on my right hip. (I sleep on my side.) In front of me appeared a fat, short sailor with a scruffy red beard and rotting teeth. He was wearing a red and white horizontal-striped shirt, a toque, and boots. His breath was foul. I told him to "Go away, you are dead. Besides, I am not that kind of girl!" (The hotel had been a brothel long ago.) The sailor was far from a large body of water in the mountains of Colorado; he was there to make his fortune and fun. He hadn't even noticed there was already a man sleeping in my bed.

Another time in Creede, I was sitting outside on the ground and enjoying the scenery. I witnessed a gunfight between two men over a woman outside a tent which served as a saloon. They shot each other. I could see their spirits rise from their dead bodies.

Scenario 2

Bob and I are both aficionados of American history. We visited many of the major battle sites of the Civil War as well as antebellum homes, particularly in Louisiana, when we were living in Houston.

I saw a young, aristocratic man, with yellow hair, in a light blue suit, ruffled white shirt and floppy black tie hanging from a tree in front of the Myrtles Plantation in St. Francisville, Louisiana (near Baton Rouge). The Myrtles is one of the most haunted of antebellum homes. It was built in 1796, has been featured on several television programs, and is now a bread and breakfast inn.

Although the tour guides had not heard of the hanging man I saw, Chloe, a slave mistress of a master, haunts the house. She had been hanged from that very tree, minus her left ear. The ear was cut off after she was found eavesdropping on a private conversation in the big house.

Scenario 3

While I was the librarian in one of the schools in Houston, I could not understand why the principal obviously disliked me and offered no support to my position in the school.

One night after midnight, as I was sitting alone in the family room of our townhouse, this vision came to me. As a young girl, my father was the owner and master of my family's plantation. The image of a black woman, like the picture on Aunt Jemima's syrup, came to me of Mammy. (I mean no disrespect; she was my caregiver, and her name was Mammy.)

Mammy and my father had a son born of their affair. She could not understand why he did not inherit the plantation. I inherited it. In that lifetime, I supposedly had the power; she had the power in this lifetime as my supervisor. Once I understood why there was friction this time around, I was able to bless the situation and our roles in each other's lives.

I had been given a non-descript job evaluation by her. In my estimation, I was doing a better-than-average job, bringing money into the school with grants I had won. I asked for an appointment to see her. I pointed out that with the evaluation, I would be ineligible for the teacher career ladder which meant receiving $1,500 more (I think) a year in pay. To my surprise, she changed the evaluation to a more favorable one. Apparently our karma was balanced. She unexpectedly transferred to another school at the end of the year. I spent my final year there serving under another principal.

Scenario 4

I spent several hours on tour at Gettysburg withdrawn and crying, so intense was the psychic imprint and my sensitivity of being able to hear, see and smell what had taken place there. Men were screaming, bleeding, moaning, dying, and dead. Cannons were firing; I could hear the booms and smell the smoke. It was pandemonium, the bloodiest battle of the Civil War, fought July 1-3, 1863, with an estimated 51,112 total casualties (killed, wounded, missing or captured). A psychic imprint often appears as a continuously running film loop when there has been great trauma in an area. Sensitives like myself are able to experience the horror of the time gone by as if it were happening in present time in front of us.

Scenario 5

I feel an association with Native American history. Before visiting the site of "Custer's Last Stand" (the Battle of Little Bighorn), fought in 1876 in Montana, I was seeing an image of a Native American maiden, surrounded by trees, with a deer nearby. When we drove into the area of the battlefield, the land looked barren and flat, with a few small hills. Then I noticed the river, surrounded by trees, in the distance.

I believe I was a young girl who was killed in that battle. When I asked the ranger guide about the number of Native American women and children killed, he said eight. Casualities among the natives were difficult to access since their dead were carried from the battlefield and buried. One report I read said that Custer had penetrated and attacked the village.

Custer's 7th Cavalry consisted of about 650 men, but he had assigned them into three units. He was unaware that the Lakota Sioux and Cheyenne encampment was estimated to be about 1,800 warriors plus family members. The other companies who were to meet Custer either retreated or did not come when expected. It is estimated that 267 of Custer's men were killed, and 51 were wounded.

The Sioux were fighting for their land in the Black Hills of what is now South Dakota, knew the layout of the land, hid in a dry creek bed and over a ridge, to conceal their numbers. The dead cavalry soldiers were scalped; Custer was not. He was one of the last men killed.

Scenario 6

When we were visiting former Houston friends in Coeur d'Alene, Idaho, I awoke one night to see a tribe of 12 Native Americans standing around the bed—a chief, warriors, women and children. Bob and I had planned a visit for the next day to see the site of a treaty between the Indians and a settler who wanted land to build a mill. There was a short walking path that ended at a large stone which commemorated the transaction many years before.

I felt an immense sadness standing there. I asked Bob to go to the car and told him that I would be there soon. I sat on the ground and meditated, apologizing to the natives for the white men who killed them, stole their land, polluted their streams, brought "civilization" with its disease and desecration of highways, noise of airplanes overhead, and trash to their once sacred land. Tears rolled down my cheeks. I was flanked by a warrior on each side of me. I asked the spirits to go in peace, to go toward the light. They would be guided to a better place.

On my way back to the car, I knew my experience was true. On the same path upon which we had walked, there lay a large feather which was not there when we came in. It was a touching sign from the natives. About a mile down the road while we were driving in the car, there was a large sign for a reservation casino. The sign had a picture of a mandala (like a dream catcher) with leather and feathers as further confirmation of our exchange.

Scenario 7

I am an empath. I can pick up feelings that are not my own, but those of others. The first time I remember it happening was after I had retired and before I moved to Charlotte. I had gone to upstate New York to visit daughter Donna. When I went, it happened to be Labor Day weekend when her father held his annual corn roast at the hunting camp. I was invited. I was walking in the surrounding woods, enjoying being in nature. My mood was good until I began to feel a pain of loneliness which I could not explain. When I got back to camp, I realized I was "picking up" on my ex-husband's feelings. When I was leaving, he was solicitous of me, sending a cousin to walk me to my rental car. I was touched by his caring.

Scenario 8

At one time, I had a spontaneous regression to a lifetime with Pat during the Civil War period. This is the scene I saw in my mind's eye: We were sitting under a tree, in love, with Pat's head in my lap. I was wearing a voluminous blue skirt.

In the next scene, I was sitting at my vanity, crying. My hair had long dark curls, and I was wearing a long black dress. I was in mourning. My husband had been shot in the chest and killed while fighting for the confederacy. We lived on a plantation in the south. There was a girl child, about five years old, standing beside me saying, "Mommy, what's wrong?"

I find it interesting that in this lifetime, we were again husband and wife. While we were married, Pat was not complimentary of southerners. Now he IS one, living in Georgia with his wife and their adopted children. Elaine and Pat adopted Elaine daughter's children, a boy and girl. I admire them both for taking on a big responsibility in their later years.

Scenario 9

I also had a spontaneous regression when being married to Bob. We had a vineyard in Italy. I am not certain of the year. I see us looking at the rows of grapes, after a long day of working the crop. It is dusk, and the sun is setting. In the next scene, I see myself serving dinner. Bob and our three children are at the table. I'll have more to say later about lifetimes with the same souls.

Scenario 10

Mother made her transition on March 24, 2002. She had double bi-pass heart surgery on her 82nd birthday, a Thursday. I was living in Houston and had gone to Taylor to be with her. I slept at her house in the antique bed which had been in my mother's family for many years. During the night of the day of the surgery, she appeared to me in a long, white gown, saying, three times, "I am going; I am going; I am going." I was puzzled about the dream.

When I visited her in the hospital the next day, I told her I would be back to take care of her the following week, spring break. She was feeling better, her blood pressure was up. I went back to Houston to pack.

On Sunday afternoon, at 4:40 in the afternoon, I got a telephone call from the cardiologist. Mother had passed away. Her heart gave out. Sunday was the third day after the surgery. She had stopped to say goodbye and let me know she was leaving. I cry now as I write of that time.

So why have I shared the scenarios above? It is to illustrate that we are all connected in a universal "collective unconscious," a term coined by the 20th century Swiss psychologist Carl Jung. It was Jung who brought focus to the forms/models of psychological inheritance which contain the knowledge and experiences we share as a species and how those archetypes impact the purpose of our life. We share in the mind of humanity throughout the ages. We are one and our connections to one another do not end with physical death.

The idea of archetypes goes back to ancient Greece with Plato (c. 400 B.C.) and his reference to forms. Jung expanded on Plato's ideas. In Caroline Myss's *Sacred Contracts* (Harmony Books: 2001), she lists and explains 73 archetypes and how you can "use your personal archetypes to help you find out what you are here on earth to learn and whom you are meant to meet," to clarify your purpose.

Myss, a medical intuitive, encourages us to identify our personal archetypes, which may be as many as twelve. I identify with eleven in my life. I have colorful book flags on each of the eleven entries in her book. For a librarian, dog-earing pages is like listening to chalk screeching across a blackboard. With flags, I can find each entry without desecrating a book.

I have not studied the topic sufficiently to understand archetypal astrology and discern how each archetype fits into a particular house in the wheel of my natal chart. To complement the *Contracts* book, Myss has published an *Archetype Cards Guidebook* (Hay House, Inc.: 2003) with 80 cards that list "light" and "shadow" attributes on each card. Directions are given for using the cards.

One of my favorite authors, Sylvia Browne, says that when times get tough during the carrying out of our contracts, we had not read the fine print. How true.

I mentioned the relationships with my two husbands and the principal. It is my belief that I signed up with these persons and members of my family on the other side, before physical birth, for the lessons and experiences I chose to encounter, enjoy, overcome, or repeat. It is logical to me that I had another chance to "make the right decisions" with my free will.

I wish to identify the following books which I have found helpful in formulating my metaphysical beliefs over the years:

Reincarnation

Moody, Raymond, M.D. *Life after Life* (Phoenix Press: 1975)

Taylor, Sandra Anne. *The Hidden Power of Your Past Lives* (Hay House, Inc.: 2011)

This book plays an important role which will be mentioned in the last chapter, "Life Now." Ms. Taylor identifies six major reasons why people choose to incarnate. The reason which fits me most closely is a life of service. She also mentions that when we have a difficult childhood, Self-Love is a part of our life's lessons.

Weiss, Brian L., M.D. *Many Lives, Many Masters* (Simon & Schuster: 1988)

Life between Lives

Browne, Sylvia. *Life on the Other Side: A Psychic's Tour of the Afterlife* (Penguin Putnam, Inc.: 2000)

Newton, Michael, Ph.D. *Journey of Souls: Case Studies of Life between Lives* (Llewellyn Publications: 1994)

Near Death Experiences (NDEs)

Alexander, Eben, M.D. *Proof of Heaven: A Neurosurgeon's Journey into the Afterlife* (Simon and Schuster: 2012)

Dr. Alexander suffered from a brain-eating bacterial infection and was in a coma for a week. He had been a skeptical scientist before his experience. When he woke up, he had total recall of his experiences on the other side. He has founded a non-profit organization merging science and spirituality. Check out his website at www.eternea.com.

Brinkley, Dannion with Paul Perry. *Secrets of the Light* (HarperCollins: 2008)

This book is my favorite of his three books on NDEs. I met Dannion when he spoke in Denver, Colorado. In 1975, Dannion was struck by lightning while on the telephone and declared clinically dead. His second NDE was during heart surgery to repair the damage from the strike. His third was when holes were drilled in his skull to relieve pressure on his brain.

His life was changed from being a bully to becoming a hospice volunteer for over 30 years and founding an organization called "Twilight Brigade" which helps dying veterans cross over.

I wore my hospice volunteer badge to his talk. He noticed, and autographed my/his book with "P.S. Great work."

A few years ago, Eric Roberts (Julia's brother) played Dannion in a television special.

Morse, Melvin, M.D. with Paul Perry. *Where God Lives: The Science of the Paranormal and How Our Brains Are Linked to the Universe* (Cliff Street Books/HarperCollins: 2000)

Dr. Morse is a pediatrician who documented NDEs in children. His subsequent studies of the brain revealed that the right temporal lobe of the brain is the site of the "God Spot" which "brings meaning and purpose to our lives." He also says that intuition is the normal function of the temporal lobe.

It was a revelation to read that depressed people get pancreatic cancer. While it was no surprise (I had been on anti-depressants for years), I found his statement interesting. He also said that NDEs, love, and positive thinking heal.

Other Resources

Burnham, Sophy. *The Art of Intuition: Cultivating Your Inner Wisdom* (Jeremy P. Tarcher/Penguin: 2011)

A few inspiring quotes from Ms. Burnham's book: "…the more you love, the more psychic and intuitive you become." "Just as meditation offers peace and serenity, it also sharpens intuition."

In Chapter 11, there is a discussion of the four types of brain waves which are measured in hertz. Theta and delta, the lowest, are the most "beneficial for developing empathy, compassion, spirituality, intuition and healing." Let's get a good night's sleep.

Cohen, Sherry Suib. *Looking for the Other Side* (Clarkson Potter Publishers: 1999). Foreword by Deepak Chopra.

Ms. Cohen was a skeptical journalist, who set out on a search for the spirit of her mother who had passed, by experiencing paranormal practices and practitioners which she describes in 2-6 shaded pages of background on each for readers new to the topic.

She comes to the conclusion "…don't look for any excuses to dismiss what can't be measured by science. Be something in between gullible and skeptical: be open-minded."

Dillard, Sherrie. *Discover Your Psychic Type: Developing and Using Your Natural Intuition* (Llewellyn Publications: 2008)

Take a simple 52-question test to find out which of four types of intuitive you are: physical, emotional, mental, or spiritual and how to develop the unique talents of each. My type is emotional, and I …"travel the path of the heart. I am "…driven by the desire for transcendental love, connection, passion, and service to others." I "…can heal and lift our hearts." My gifts are "compassion and unconditional love."

I will bullet ways in which I have shown "moxie"—courage/nerve/guts:

- Leaving two marriages which were no longer working for me

- Conquering pancreatic cancer

- Moving across country alone (to Houston; back to Houston; to Charlotte)

- Moving nine times in eleven years in the military and setting up households

- Accepting two jobs over the telephone, sites unseen

- Hot air ballooning, with a guide, over freeways and a body of water in Houston

- Traveling alone (or in a group where I knew no one)

- Considering bungee jumping in Queenstown, NZ. I decided it was not worth $100 to throw off pressure in my eyeballs; wretch my back; or find that the rope to which my feet were attached was too long, swinging into rocks or plunging into the river below.

- Enjoying zip-lining in South Carolina

- Handling life's daily challenges with only myself to rely on

- Writing to CEOs when there is a problem. I have the reference skills to find their names and addresses

- Being involved in social justice activities for those less fortunate

- Whooping it up while being driven in a jet boat in a steep canyon in New Zealand. 360-degree wheelies were a blast

- Trusting the Mountain Man when white-water rafting in Colorado

- Serving as a hospice volunteer. Not every person can do it

- Taking responsibility for my health decisions, along with my doctors

I have been richly blessed by the Universe with the gifts of intuition and moxie. I pray that I use them wisely.

10.

Trust and Love

*W*hat is trust? There are several definitions in the dictionary. I choose to define trust as our expectation and reliance on the integrity of a person to be truthful. It is/should be the foundation on which relationships are based.

A couple of months ago, the minister of my church gave a sermon on the topic of trust. He referenced Robert C. Solomon's book *Spirituality for the Skeptic: The Thoughtful Love of Life* (Oxford University Press: 2002). Judging by the title of the book, it was not one I would likely have picked up to read. But I did read and examine Chapter 3, Spirituality As Cosmic Trust.

Solomon says that "trust implies dependency and vulnerability" and describes the following types of trust:

- *Basic:"*…security in one's own existence and confidence in one's place in the world. Basic trust gets established—or destroyed—very early in life."

- *Cosmic:* "…emotional sense of being secure in the world."

- *Authentic:* "…trusting in the face of uncertainty and lack of control, accepting…whatever happens. In authentic trust, we decide to trust. Trusting is a choice."

- *Unconditional:* akin to trust in God.

- *Simple:* "naïve trust, trust as yet unchallenged, unquestioned."

- *Blind:* "stubborn, obstinate, possibly even self-deluding; one refuses to be surprised."

In the above chapter, Solomon also discusses betrayal and forgiveness. The chapter is thirteen pages in length and is philosophical; however, it serves to define different types of trust.

He also says that "forgiving is not the same as forgetting."

I identify with the prior sentence. Although I have forgiven my father, ex-husband and former close friends, memories remain. Granted, I do not dwell on those memories, but they have resurfaced during the writing of this manuscript. Once trust has been betrayed, I would be reluctant to trust those individuals in a future relationship with me.

In 1996, when I was a hospice volunteer for two years in Colorado, I considered studying to become a hospice chaplain. I signed up for a class called "Clinical Observation," one of the first courses required in that ministry field.

The instructor was no-nonsense, likeable Rev. Pam. She turned us students inside-out, forcing us to face our own issues before we would be able to help others deal with theirs. We delved into genealogy and family patterns for generations.

I had a glaring issue with trust. It probably dated back to not having developed basic trust in my childhood. When Pam and I discussed my problem, she said, "Perhaps there have been persons in your life who were not worthy of your trust." Wham!

As students, we visited patients, some of them church members, in the hospital, hospice and nursing homes, and were evaluated on our reported interactions. I don't know why I remember the date, but on July 31, I awoke knowing that being a hospice chaplain was not the path I was meant to travel.

For the remainder of this chapter, I will focus on the topic of Love. Over this lifetime, I have had opportunities to learn and grow in this area. As I mentioned in the Introduction, the third component of loving will be revealed in the final chapter (no surprises).

One of the books I read before I thought about writing this memoir (which was helpful in choosing the theme of this book) is by Barbara De Angelis, Ph.D. *How Did I Get Here? Finding Your Way to Renewed Hope and Happiness When Life and Love Take Unexpected Turns* (St. Martin's Press: 2005). Hers is an inspirational, readable book offering techniques for understanding life lessons and using the challenges as a springboard for regeneration. It helped me accept the past four, difficult years of my life.

Gary Chapman has published a series of books on love languages. Knowing the ways love is expressed or received gives us ideas for optimal results. The book which I read was *The Five Love Languages for Singles (Northfield Publishing:* 2004). Included in the book is a thirty-question profile for identifying primary and secondary love languages. The five areas are words of affirmation; gifts; acts of service; quality time; and physical touch. My #1 language of love is physical touch, which, for a period of four years, I was able to feed through the Sunday hugs of Unity Church congregation members. I have been under chiropractic care for years, and that helps, although it does not take the place of having a partner's touch. My secondary language is quality time which I have not been experiencing in a close relationship.

This chapter is the perfect one for telling my stories about angels. Angels are the epitome of Agape, unconditional love. It is not so much that I *believe* in angels is that I *know* there are angels available to assist me and everyone if we only ask. I will tell some of the inter-action I have had with these divine beings and offer a list of books which you may find helpful to read if you are so inclined. I will give a short background on some of the select few I have included. There are also websites listed.

The first story, which happened about a month ago, involves a "lost" debit card. I was frantic after having looked EVERYWHERE for it, (although I did skip looking in the freezer). I asked my angels, more than once, to help me locate it. About a week later, I was in the

Book Rack, purchasing a used book. When I opened my purse—one of the first places I looked in every nook and cranny—there was the "lost" card which had slipped down to the bottom of a narrow pocket, where I thought I had checked. I got into a discussion with the clerk (witness) about the situation. I said, out loud to the angels, "I asked you to help me find it." I am clairaudient and heard the reply, "We heard you" and then something about my wanting the opportunity to stop the hysterical drama and do what I needed to do. And that was to go to the bank, report the card missing, and order a new one—which I did days earlier. When I got home, I cut up the original card, but did remember to thank the angels for helping me to find it.

One of the ways I know that my angels are sending me affirming messages is that of finding coins, pennies mostly. Just before Christmas, I saw a 54" lighted angel advertised in a Big Lots store. I had given the spiral, modern trees for display outside my house for the holiday season to my neighbor, who was delighted to receive them. The trees had become too complicated for me, with the hip pain, to construct. I purchased the large angel and placed her inside the trunk of my car. I drove about 100 feet in the shopping center to the next store. When I stepped out of my car, there were two pennies laying at my feet in the parking lot. I always say, when finding a coin, "Find a penny, pick it up. Have good luck." Then I put it in my wallet. The angels approved of my purchasing a symbol of their presence.

Last May, when I was downsizing in anticipation of a move, I found another penny outside my home. I said, "Thanks, angels. Now I am ready for quarters." To show they do listen, and with a sense of humor, they produced a quarter inside a soup bowl on a top shelf in a kitchen cabinet that I was clearing. There was little chance that there would be a quarter there, and I would find it, without angels placing it there.

Last week when I was walking in the mall parking lot on my way to have lunch, I was planning how to market my book when it is published. No sooner than I had the thought, I looked down and found another two pennies and picked them up. Again, it was an affirmation that there will be success. I trust that angels are supportive of us, and that we each have them. Their purpose is to help and affirm us on our journey.

A couple of weeks ago, I was struggling to balance my checkbook. I know that my daughters just look online to determine the bank's balance in their accounts. I do some on-line banking, but I am old-fashioned enough to think the account should balance each month by checking off the cleared checks, adding any deposits not yet accounted for, and subtracting the checks and debits still outstanding. I had re-checked all the subtractions in the check register. I kept the books and balanced bank statements for the family business when I was in high school. My mother taught me how to do the procedure, and I was good at it. I have always kept the check book in my marriages and in my life as a single.

I was entirely frustrated when I could not find the $30+ error. That was not acceptable to me. I went to the bank and asked one of the officers for assistance. He said that was not his job. I asked him to do me a favor. He went over some of the work on the statement and checkbook, not locating the problem. He had an appointment with a client, so I picked up my papers and went out the door. I spent more time trying to find what was wrong. I began crying, pleading with my angels to help me find the error. I was totally discouraged. I persevered and learned that I had marked off a check on the statement, but neglected to put a red check next to the listing in the register. Therefore, I had counted it as still outstanding, when it had already cleared. I use colored ink for different functions and place a checkmark on top of each page when all items are in. I expressed gratitude to my angels for their help in spite of the stress I had caused myself.

I admit I express doubt sometimes when I do not receive immediate assistance. I know that I am forgiven because angels are unconditional love and, I believe, they know our struggles on this planet and have compassion for us.

About four years ago, I had a life script reading by a rotund, jovial, loving Santa look-alike named Carl. Carl and his wife were visiting Unity Church and were available for private consultations. Carl is a dowser, one who used a rod to obtain answers and information from spirit guides. Whoa...; actually, he was skilled in its use. His was like no other psychic reading I have experienced over the years. He said that I had two guides, a master teacher which I had attracted, and numerous angels (I need not give the specific number here) who assist me on my journey. We accessed the Hall of Records (Akashic) on the other side to view what I came to accomplish in this life and the skills I had brought with me.

I realize that the above scenario may seem unbelievable to many, but the experience was real to me. It helped me to know that I am not alone each day. I can ask for spiritual help, and I do so.

I am aware of "psychic hotlines." I would not encourage their use in seeking spiritual guidance. Some of the companies are profit-making schemes to keep you on the telephone line as long as possible. The "psychics" give generalized information which could apply to anyone. I prefer my readings to be done in person so that I can sense a connection to the other person. On minimal occasions, I have had a sight unseen communication with someone who has been recommended. We are fortunate in Charlotte to have a monthly metaphysical magazine which features articles on holistic topics and has a listing of practitioners in the last pages.

I have found that the tapes or CDs some readers provide to be helpful. A couple of days ago, I replayed a tape that my friend Sal had done on June 15, 2012. She was "right on" in what is happening even now. Sal does not predict things like "This will happen in two weeks." She does what I call a "soul" reading by tuning into the energy of where you are emotionally. She has confirmed my own directional thinking without my giving her any information beforehand.

Some of my favorite angel books are:

Browne, Sylvia. *Sylvia Browne's Book of Angels* (Hay House, Inc.: 2003)

Sylvia's book is exquisitely and powerfully illustrated by Christina Simonds.

Sylvia is my favorite, prolific author. She had written over 50 books before her passing on November 20, 2013. Although her physical light has gone from the planet, her spiritual light lives on through her books. I have nineteen of her books on my personal library shelves, and have read additional titles of hers. The lady writes with a no-nonsense, humorous approach. She knew from a young age that she had psychic ability. She channeled her spirit guide, Francine, and was a frequent guest on the Montel Williams television program. She founded the Society of Novus Spiritus church in California.

Sylvia's book is comprehensive, listing the ten phyla of angels, their purpose and function. She is a strong proponent of the existence and assistance of angels in our lives.

Kim O'Neill has written *How to Talk with Your Angels* (HarperCollins: 1995)

Kim is a psychic channeler who lives in Houston, Texas. I met her during a presentation shortly after Mother passed in 2002. Kim told me that Mother was beside me saying, "I like your hair." She also told me that I would be an author.

Kim has since written *The Calling: My Journey with the Angels* (A.R.E.: 2012).

Kim is a soft spoken, enthusiastic, strawberry blonde lady. If you enter a search of "Kim O'Neill You Tube," you can watch a ten-minute interview of her speaking about her work of purpose and service.

An angel guru extraordinaire is Doreen Virtue, Ph.D. who has written over 50 books and other media on angel topics. Her *Angel Numbers 101* (Hay House, Inc.:2008) tells how angels communicate with us through repeating number sequences. She gives channeled messages as to sequences we notice in telephone numbers, on license plate numbers, clocks, etc. Recently, I have been seeing three fours (444) repeatedly which means that I am "loved, supported, and guided by Heavenly beings and have nothing to fear." Every time I see the ubiquitous yellow cab around town with the telephone number 704-444-4444, I thank the angels for their message.

In Doreen's *Archangels and Ascended Masters: A Guide to Working and Healing with Divinities and Deities* (Hay House, Inc.: 2003), she lists 77 divinities from many cultures and how they can help us with life's problems. I have been calling upon, for many months, Archangel Raphael for his healing abilities (for humans and animals) to restore health to my left hip. The book is well-organized, and the deities are listed alphabetically for ease of reference.

Doreen's website is www.angeltherapy.com. Particularly helpful is a list, by state, of certified angel therapy practitioners trained by Doreen. Charlotte has three, one of whom is a member of my former church.

In a similar vein to Doreen's Angel Numbers book is the website www.sacredscribes.net. Joanne is a psychic medium who hosts this site. There is an extensive list of information on esoteric topics in which you may be interested.

One of the most intriguing books by a former self-avowed skeptic is by Gary E. Schwartz, Ph.D. *The Sacred Promise: How Science is Discovering Spirits' Collaboration with Us in Our Daily Lives* (Simon & Schuster, Inc.: 2011). The Forward to the book is written by John Edward, psychic medium. Dr. Schwartz is a professor, educator, author and scientist at the University of Arizona where he conducted numerous double-blind experiments to determine whether spirits exist. Although the book is scientifically-based, it is readable. I wish to quote from the book's back jacket:

> "*The Sacred Promise* (is) an exploration into the world of spirits, where more than just data and theories are offered, but actual evidence of an active and helpful spiritual world is revealed. Be it the deceased, angels, or spirit guides, these beings do exist and are reaching out to help us in our day-to-day lives."

There is an extensive list of recommended readings in the above book.

Angels are my (sometimes unseen) friends, confidants who, when I ask, provide me with guidance through the vicissitudes of life. Many of our conversations are done telepathically; at other times, I hear them inside my head. They are my therapists, and only ask gratitude as a fee. I don't even have to lay on a couch to talk and listen to them.

I have eleven images of angels in my home, in various rooms. There were even more angels in the decorations at Christmas. I am sitting with an "I believe in angels" pillow supporting me as I write. Some images of angels are large, 3-4 feet high, and have names. Anya is in my bedroom watching over me as I sleep. Garda is in my backyard garden watching the birds, and an occasional squirrel, dipping into the birdbath for a drink or quick shower in the heat of summer. I love inanimate creatures, too, and name them. Scamper is my gray squirrel. Nearby are bunny Fluffy and her baby, Fluffette, on mom's back.

Because I am sensitive to energy and had various spirits, some menacing and some merely curious, waking me with their presence (sometimes with a scream from me) in the middle of the night, I often ask my angels to keep them out of my bedroom when I am sleeping. I have boundaries and one of those is that I need my rest undisturbed.

11.
Life Now

It is mid-November. As I was walking to my car this week, an image began forming in my head along with an unfolding story. I am driving a careening chariot, which is drawn by two spirited horses, in a race. The bumps are coming frequently, and the chariot is threatening to overturn. My GPS is broken, and I am blind in my left eye. I then notice a Ben Hur lookalike by my side who is offering to drive. He looks strong and capable. I turn the reins over to him. The bumps still come, but the chariot remains upright. When my ego asserts itself to take over the reins again, the chariot returns to its former state when I was driving. So the scenario goes for the remainder of the race, a life time.

What a message my angels have given me. God is the expert Charioteer. He needs to be the One driving. When I think I am in charge, chaos reigns. I need to let go and let God. He knows the plan for my life, where I am going, and how to get there in one piece.

I test myself to see if I heed the message. God does not test to punish us. In reality, I am driving in my car, approaching an intersection and slowing down to about 5 mph. My purse slips from my lap. I do not reach down to pick it up, but my attention is diverted for perhaps two seconds. Bam! I connect with the back bumper of the Lexus in front of me; her car's front bumper slides under the SUV in front of her, causing the only damage in the accident. It is fortunate that no one is hurt. The passenger in the lady's car is her daughter whom she was bringing home from having cancer radiation.

We three drivers pull over and get out of our cars to exchange necessary information. The gentleman in the SUV has a cell phone and calls the South Carolina police to fill out a report. My first reaction when I get out of the car is fear. I have car insurance (for perhaps thirty years with the same company) without a single accident on my record. Because I am on a fixed income, I cannot afford a rise in my rates. We get back into our cars because it is cold and windy outside. It takes 25 minutes for the officer to arrive. I knew I would be late for my chiropractor's appointment. I do not own a cell phone for a number of reasons. I am normally a punctual person.

As the drama begins to build in me, I ask the angels to handle the situation. I am not capable at the time. I eventually become calm as I get out of my car and tap on the daughter's window. She looks at me quizzically but rolls down her window. I apologize for the accident, which undoubtedly adds to her stress, and tell her I am sorry she has to undergo radiation. She has three weeks remaining with the treatment. I tell her that I did not have radiation, but that I did undergo chemo for six months with the pancreatic cancer. We chat for a few moments, and I return to my car.

The officer arrives. It takes 35 minutes to enter our data in the computer and give us each a copy. An hour is spent from start to finish. How can I be so exact? I take notes on the available paper, my cards with my personal information, two of which I give to the other drivers for them to record information.

I explain to the chiropractor and his staff why I am late for the appointment. Fortunately, there is no late charge for not giving prior notification.

The trauma of the day was not enough. I had to deal with aftermath the next day. I had the attitude it had to be done, so I called my insurance company, got their fax number, went to Staples and had the report faxed. I was given a citation by the officer, so I had to go to the bank and get a mail order for the amount of the fine, and then off to the never-empty line at the post office to send a certified letter (additional expense) to the CCT (court trial) Office. The court would be a 61-mile round trip to appear for the summons, so I chose the option to mail the fine, having made copies of all the paperwork for my pendaflex "Citation" file. Because I had the experience of being in education for numerous years, I make copies in case there is any dispute.

I then treated myself to lunch at Applebee's with my favorite tomato basil soup and oriental salad with extra dressing on the side.

For the past two years, I never fail when I strap myself into the seatbelt in my car to say, "Angels, protect Natalie (my car, Natalie Nissan) and me; keep us safe." While I am saying the prayer, I am encircling the car and myself with a spiral of the white light of protection. On the first outing in the car each day, I also say, "My Spiritual Family (angels, master teacher, and spirit guides), raise my vibration to its highest level so that I may be who I truly am and help others to be who they truly are." The angels and others must have been on coffee break at 2:15 P.M. last Tuesday, the day of the accident.

Regarding my life now, I am most fortunate to have both daughters living here in Charlotte. Donna lives six doors down from me in the cul-de-sac; Rhonda lives 5 miles away. They are amazing young women with kind, generous hearts. Donna has been a massage therapist, and is a nurse who works in data informatics for a Fortune 500 company involved in the betterment of health care. She loves her work and puts in overtime for the job. Rhonda is a college graduate who was in the mortgage business for a time and now works for an agency which specializes in travel to Italy. They are each single and are career women.

Donna has two green thumbs (figuratively), loves plants, flowers and gardening. She has an ability to rescue a shamrock plant from the jaws of death. Our personalities are much alike, and we both have psychic experiences. Rhonda is the social butterfly, has many friends (24 of us for Thanksgiving at her house), is a gourmet cook, and travels anywhere in the world if she has 20 minutes to pack. Both girls are animal lovers: Donna, dogs and cats; Rhonda, cats. I am extremely proud of each of them and am honored to be their Mother.

Another important person (although 800 miles distant in New York state) is my dear friend Joy whom I have known since the early 1970's. She was the librarian at a pharmaceutical company in Rouses Point when I was filling in for a lady in one of the departments who was on maternity leave. We became fast friends personally, and as couples with our husbands. When I left Rouses Point in 1981 for Houston, Texas, our contact became less frequent, but continued.

Joy's mom, Ann, is quite the trooper. I met her those many years ago. Joy is her mother's caregiver. Her mom has a clever wit. I always liked her and felt welcome in her home. She would need her wits about her with raising six children.

Joy's husband passed in 2010. We picked up our friendship where we had left off. She visited me in Charlotte perhaps three years ago and treated us to lobster, our favorite food. She has been my rock these past four years. We are always there for each other with frequent telephone calls, e-mails, snail mail, cards, laughter, sympathy, etc. She has supported me during my worst times and continues to cheerfully answer her telephone even when she knows it is me with a long-winded story. I trust that I am there for her as well.

I began this manuscript less than four months ago. It is now the end of February, and I am completing this final chapter. Now that I have received my tax refund, I will contract a tech person to help me with the photos. Words flow freely from me; I flee freely from tech issues beyond my expertise.

I divided the opus into chapters and worked (often at 2:A.M. when I awake many days) on different ones, rarely in numerical number. It took a long time for me to complete Chapter 5 because it was the most emotionally difficult.

To give this chapter (Life Now) organization, I will summarize the next sections into social, physical, mental, emotional, and spiritual areas and what is transpiring in each.

Socially, when I first arrived in Charlotte, I became active in church programs, classes, courses, events in the newspaper, the senior center, yoga, contract bridge, etc. I am a social individual and am energized when I am around most others. Since the limitation with my physical health at this time, I have cut down on many activities, keeping the ones at church, and Senior Scholars, once a week. I go to movies and spend time, when she is available, with Donna. I have many acquaintances, but no close friends here in Charlotte. This Cancerian crab lady has retreated into her shell this past fall and winter to reflect and heal. I do get out of the house daily for lunch, errands, and an occasional social activity.

I miss my volunteer work with hospice due to the hip injury and not being able to stand/walk easily for a three-hour shift. I have no doubt I will return to that organization when I am physically healed. To show the work's importance to me, I am including an article I wrote recently for a hospice blog.

What does being a hospice volunteer mean to me? It means supporting persons and families who may be confused, stressed, fearful and/or sad in this life situation. It means being respectful of the stage (according to Dr. Kubler-Ross) where the patient and family are in the process of grief, even if it means they have not gotten past the stage of anger.

I have known pain and depression; I can empathize with some of the emotions they may be experiencing. I am part of an extraordinary team who find working in hospice their life's work. Everyone cannot, or does not wish, to assist persons who are dying. I can, and do.

I do not fear death. If the subject arises in conversation, I can be reassuring to the patient without trying to convince him/her. Hospice is "about" the patient, not me. It is reflective listening and being a loving presence in the patient's life. Of all the volunteer work I could be doing, I choose hospice in which to make a difference.

Physically, I have made progress over the past months. In January of 2014, I learned from my oncologist that I remain free of pancreatic cancer into year three—that's the biggie. I described, in Chapter 8, some of the therapies for the hip problem. I have added other experiences to deal with the hip pain, stomach upset, and headaches in addition to taking OTC (over-the-counter) drugs. Some OTC pain relievers are film-coated. Taking these lessen the stomach distress. I also discovered that drinking more water (hydrating) has lessened the severity and frequency of headaches—particularly those which felt like a spear had been thrown into my left eye socket.

I had a Reiki energy treatment at Unity last week, my first. I will be going again tomorrow. The fee is by donation to have four trained energy healers lay their hands gently on areas of my body, not just the hip area. I could feel the heat coming from their hands. The heat from one person's hands was so intense that I felt her perspiration on my face and head. The session lasted about 30 minutes. I was told to drink large amounts of water to flush toxins from my system. What I was not told, and I don't mean to be indelicate, was that I should remain within bathroom distance for 24 hours—the toxins liquefy product and it does insist on coming out. There has been more relief from discomfort. I will continue the weekly treatments for as long as I am in Charlotte.

The most astounding therapy happened on January 23, 2014, when, after having read Sandra Taylor's *The Hidden Power of Your Past Lives* (mentioned in Chapter 9), I had an appointment with Linda, a clinical hypnotherapist/regression therapist. Her credentials are impressive. The idea of cellular memory--that we carry wounds/pain from one lifetime to another--is not new to me. I had read of it years before, perhaps in one of Sylvia Browne's books. I know it to be true from my experiences.

Within the 90 minute session, Linda regressed me back into three lifetimes, two of which I had experienced prior images of but did not know what happened before or after the scenes I witnessed. I believe the first lifetime we visited was the source lifetime of my left side and hip problem. It is in ancient Rome. I am a young, aristocrat soldier in uniform. My hands are tied, and I am being dragged by two horses with a chariot attached. There is a burly, evil-looking man who is driving the chariot. Periodically, he relieves the horses from his long whip and uses it on my almost lifeless body. I am bloodied; dust encrusted; twisted; and have broken bones from hitting rocks on the path. I can see myself on my left side while being dragged. I died from the injuries I received. Linda took me back to before that scene (the one image of which I had no prior knowledge.) I was on trial in front of the ruling patrician class for speaking out about the social injustice laws toward slaves and others. I was sentenced to death by dragging.

The second lifetime (of which I had a prior image) is of a male in aristocratic robes with a green plumed hat in a prison made out of rocks. There was little light coming from a small opening with bars. I had to stoop and was unable to stand upright in the tiny space. The food was insect-ridden. It seemed that the scene was in 1500's Europe (I knew before that here was where my claustrophobia in this lifetime was exacerbated.) Again, Linda and I went to what was happening before I spent those 30 years in the hole of a dungeon made of rock.

I am a wealthy landowner. There are slaves (non-black men) working in the fields. They are being beaten by overseers. Linda asked me what I was doing. I told her I was watching, but that I turned my back and walked away. It was later that I began, once again, speaking out against injustice. For doing so, I was thrown into prison to rot. One would think, after these two lifetimes of speaking out, that I would shut my month. It appears that I am a slow learner. I continue, in this lifetime, to speak out and/or write letters to those in charge—perpetrators—when I observe injustices.

The third lifetime (of which I had a prior image) is of an old woman, swaddled in heavy, dark clothing walking down a deserted, ancient cobbled street in a city (gray buildings) in the cold. There is a crutch under her right arm, and she is dragging her left side and leg. Linda asked me when it was and where. The date 1614 came to me, and the country was Greece. Again, we went back. What was happening before this scene?

I was an older female, in a field of hay, driving two horses attached to a wagon. I was atop the hay. The horses went over rocks on the edge of the field, and I fell off the wagon, onto my left hip. It was broken. I had no money to see a doctor. Linda asked if I lived alone and how I was found. I see my husband, at our table. He comes looking for me when I was not home by dusk. (He was hungry?)

The scene on the city street is later, after my husband had died. I had lost or sold the farm and moved to the city. My left hip has been through eons of pain. It is time for it to heal.

Linda used a visualization technique to release the traumatic memories from these bodies broken over lifetimes. Near the end of the hypnosis session, Linda (she is intuitive) said that there was a being who had a message for me. I saw a large angel standing before me. Angels are androgynous (free of gender because they have no bodies), but I felt a feminine energy approaching me. She placed her hand on my heart with the message, "Be Love."

Tonight, as I was leafing through Doreen's book, mentioned in Chapter 10, under angels who help with writing and writing projects, Archangel Gabriel's name jumped off the page at me. There are different opinions about how many archangels there are—some say 4, others 7, others say an infinite number. Doreen lists 15 by name. Of those she has channeled, only 4 are female energy. Doreen uses "he or she" pronouns. It is possible that Archangel Gabriel was the one who gave me the message. I thanked her this evening for her presence and advice.

The reason I am relating these stories is because, after suffering daily, chronic pain in the 6-8.5 range (on a scale of 10) for a year and eight months, I was pain free for three days after the therapy treatment. There is still discomfort in the area, but nothing like the pain I had been suffering for so long. You may believe it or not. My experience rings true to me.

I have slept in the full-fetal sleep position for the past several months. Psychiatrist Samuel Dunkell, M.D. in his book *Sleep Positions: The Night Language of the Body* (Harmony Books: 2002) describes the four most common sleep positions as full fetal; prone; royal; and semi-fetal, as well as several more unusual positions. I find it of interest to intuit that because I need protection from threatening memories, I am in retreat and sleeping, balled into the position in the womb where all was safe and warm. You might find the book of interest to analyze your unspoken language of the night.

Mentally, I am comfortable with what is happening in this area. I read dozens of books on metaphysics (and rarely read fiction unless it is based on history), many of them mentioned in this book as resources which I have found helpful on my journey. I read a daily newspaper and the comics; I skip the sports section. I skim the headlines of the newspaper and choose not to read stories about violence and negativity. The latter two categories are the reasons I do not listen to local or national news. My career was one of being an information broker, and I continue that curiosity by doing research on topics for articles I have written for publication as well as fact-checking for this book. I am a life-long learner who takes various continuing education classes which are of interest to me. I enjoy weekly speakers prominent in the community during eight months of the year with Senior Scholars. I find the game of contract bridge challenging and hope to get back to it when I can sit for a longer period of time. I learn more about technology, mostly through trial and error. I believe if one maintains an active mind, one never grows old in spite of the passing years.

Emotionally, I am a work in progress. Some days, it is "Good Morning, God;" other days it is "Good God, Morning!" I realize that depression is a cyclical, normal happenstance for which I refuse, any longer, to take medication. There have been many side effects from prescription meds. If I need to take a take a break and lie on the couch for a day or so, I do, without shame.

Great mystics (Saint John of the Cross; Mother Teresa; Eckhart Tolle among them) have written of their "dark night of the soul." It is a period of intense suffering before peace is attained by those on a spiritual quest in their lives. The dark night is ending as I come into the light of day.

I have noticed a change in the way I react to crises in life. Generally, now I am more calm, and even though I do not want to handle some problems which inevitably surface in life (like my taxes and mortgage payment rising and my car insurance doubling recently), I ask for help from my angels and take care of the telephone call, letter, or whatever needs to be done to solve, to the best of my ability, the problem. If I cannot solve it, I am learning to accept it without the accompanying drama. A perfect example is pain. Anyone would try to lessen it, as have I. I will live with discomfort which may remain for a time. Life is for living joyfully, and that thought is something of which I remind myself.

Over a two-week period recently, I left a telephone message for three persons whom I know, not to chat, but from whom I sought information. My call was returned by not one of them. Returning a call is a courtesy, not a requirement. Emotionally, I let the situation, and them, go from my life. I am letting go of being a drama queen and am now only a drama princess on occasion.

In the manner of spirituality, Eckhart Tolle's book *The Power of Now: A Guide to Spiritual Enlightenment* (New World Library: 1997) is bringing me to live more frequently in the moment. The present moment is all there actually is; the past is gone, and the future is uncertain. Surrendering to the present moment frees us from suffering and leads to peace and wisdom. The image I had at one time was my being in a boat rowing upstream against the flow of the river. When I change the image of the boat's direction to match that of the water's flow, life becomes easier. Eckhart says that we can capture the Now by deep breathing, meditation, and conscious choice.

I spend many quiet moments alone. I meditate when I awake in the morning and before I go to sleep at night. My most comfortable position is not the lotus, but lying in bed, taking slow, deep breaths and focusing on the stillness within. The time spent in the morning gets me going for the day. The evening time prompts me to express gratitude for the gifts that I have received and appreciate throughout that day. Daily prayer is also my practice.

Another source for living in the moment is Byron Katie's *Loving What Is* (Harmony Books: 2002). Byron speaks of doing "The Work" for solving life's problems.

Being religious and being spiritual is not analogous. A person can be one, but not necessarily the other. I like the combination. I have almost always been a churchgoer. It is what works for me. As I mentioned before, I was raised Catholic, then became a Methodist.

In the past seven years, I have been a member of the Unity Church and, for the past two of those years, I have been a member who attends the Unitarian Universalist Church. The two religions have liberal orientations.

Two of Unity's core values are "Love" and "Inclusiveness." The love expressed is unconditional and the service is heart-centered. In inclusiveness, we are all one and believe that all people are created with sacred worth.

Two of Unitarian Universalism's Seven Principles are the inherent worth and dignity of every person and the goal of world community with peace, liberty and justice for all.

I greatly admire the senior ministers of both churches, Nancy of Unity and Jay of UU. Unity members are huggers, an action in which I reveled. It is a big-in-heart but small-in-number congregation, and I desired a larger church. UU has a brilliant minister and an extraordinary music program. Both churches are involved in social justice programs like Room in the Inn where homeless neighbors are fed dinner, breakfast, a bagged lunch, given transportation and a place to sleep during four winter months. UU provides this service to nine persons each week. It is for Room in the Inn that I prepare a meal or two for thirteen persons. There are nine neighbors, usually men, and four of our church members who provide service during the evening. Other members are involved in set-up, clean-up, transportation, other meals, and laundry.

I hope the Mystics and Metaphysics group continues at UU. It is a gathering of like-minded persons. There are also other groups and activities which take place at UU. The church is a leader in the community and offers opportunities to serve.

As I mentioned in Chapter 9, I have chosen a life of service. I am proud of what I have accomplished and am accomplishing. I have a loving, generous heart. Not only have I shared love with children in my career, I continue to extend love to others, to share. Just one example of the platitude "nothing says loving like something from the oven" is that I baked goodies for 26 persons during Christmas time. Some expect several goodies, others I surprise with a treat or two.

My daughters receive a basket of six assorted goodies (Rhonda hates fruitcake, so she gets double crispies.) I send boxes to my 93-year-old pen pal Lois and to three persons in the office of Edward Jones Investments in Houston. I brought goodies to the staff at hospice and the doctors and staff at the chiropractic practice; Karen, my hair dresser; Frankie, my nail person; Scott, the Assistant Manager/computer guru at Staples; favorite waitress Angie and two others at Brigs Restaurant; and the man at the jewelry store who has fixed my inexpensive jewelry a couple of times without charging me.

I have not gone into all the organizations for which I have volunteered over the years, but working with hospice patients, their families, and the staff has been one of my greatest joys and avenues of service where Love is expressed to, and received from, humanity.

And now, the big reveal for the persons who have read the book all the way through and did not turn immediately to the last chapter to learn the third component of learning and growing love. Ta-dah... it is sharing Love. I complete the trio by listing ways in which we can practice Agape, unconditional love, the highest form of love on our journey.

* * *

Ways of sharing love:

Smile, particularly at strangers and small children.

Give a compliment. It will be appreciated, and most persons will be happy you noticed something special about them.

Pray and meditate. Praying is talking to God; meditating is listening to divine guidance.

Listen to, and care about, others.

Tell someone you love them, whether it is a spouse, a relative, or a friend. You may not hear the words echoed, but you might.

Accept persons as they are and not try to change them into who you want them to be.

Give a gratuity for service received. Give a larger one for exceptional service.

Communicate, by telephoning; writing a letter; sending an e-mail; mailing a surprise package; saying "hello."

Comfort persons coping with difficulties. Be a loving presence.

Donate goods or services to a charity. There is a website, www.satruck.com, if you want a range of deductible values if you itemize on your taxes.

Support your church financially if you attend one.

Perform random kindness and senseless acts of beauty, quote attributed to Anne Herbert. Assist or cheer up someone—let them in front of you in the grocery line or while driving; tell a parent that you notice that their child is well-behaved; listen to another's story, etc. Choose your opportunity to be helpful.

Heal Mother Earth, our planet, by recycling; conserving electricity and water; grouping errands to conserve gasoline or take public transportation; planting trees and flowers; abstaining from littering; and admiring her beauty.

Share your talents whether it is cooking; singing; dancing (even if you have no partner); writing; speaking; mentoring, etc.

Be good to yourself by keeping doctors' appointments; taking vitamins and medications; exercising; taking a nap and/or a bubble bath (not at the same time); maintaining a positive attitude; and being assertive (not aggressive) when you are being verbally attacked. I told someone close that I loved myself too much to listen to abuse directed at me. If you feel there is a wrong to be righted by a business, write to the CEO of the company. I have done this numerous times over the years. Most libraries probably have the electronic Reference USA database where you can locate this information and the corporate address. Speak up against injustice.

Have integrity by being true to yourself and to others when you give your word.

Ask and allow your angels, guides, master teachers, and spirits of loved ones to help you.

Be forgiving as well as being a good friend.

Most of all, *live life joyfully* by being who you truly are — Love incarnate.

I leave you with the following quotes:

> *There comes a time in your life, when you walk away from all the drama and people who create it. You surround yourself with people who make you laugh. Forget the bad, and focus on the good. Love the people who treat you right, pray for the ones who don't. Life is too short to be anything but happy. Falling down is a part of life, getting back up is living.*
>
> *-Jose N. Harris*

> *Today may there be peace within. May you trust that you are exactly where you meant to be. May you not forget the infinite possibilities that are born of faith in yourself and others. May you use the gifts that you have received and pass on the love that has been given to you. May you be content with yourself just the way you are. Let this knowledge settle into your bones, and allow your soul the freedom to sing, dance, praise and love. It is there for each and every one of us.*
>
> *-Author Unknown*

Acknowledgements

Thank you, Kerry Beach, Tech Guru Extraordinaire, and, Brelan Boyce, FriesenPress account manager, without whose assistance this book would not be a reality.

About the Author

Dolores Eckles (a.k.a. Love Goddess-in-training) is a retired Library Media Specialist and holds Bachelor of Arts and Master's degrees in Library Science. She has worked with students in Grades K-12.

During her career, she was twice elected "Teacher of the Year" and was the recipient of twelve (of fourteen) competitive, educational grants, one of which enabled her to study in Ireland for two weeks.

Ms. Eckles, who lives in North Carolina, has traveled on six continents, is a hospice volunteer, and is a published author of three articles in medical journals.

CPSIA information can be obtained at www.ICGtesting.com
Printed in the USA
LVOW11s1622170814

399538LV00001B/10/P